HIDDEN HISTORY *of* RIDGEFIELD CONNECTICUT

HIDDEN HISTORY *of* RIDGEFIELD CONNECTICUT

Jack Sanders

THE History PRESS

Published by The History Press
Charleston, SC 29403
www.historypress.net

First published 2015

Manufactured in the United States

ISBN 978.1.46711.814.9

Library of Congress Control Number: 2015942271

Notice: The information in this book is true and complete to the best of our knowledge. It is offered without guarantee on the part of the author or The History Press. The author and The History Press disclaim all liability in connection with the use of this book.

To the many kind people who have helped me write this book and provided these pictures: thank you!

Contents

Introduction

Ridgefield's people, places and things seem to provide a never-ending source of stories, almost all of them interesting and many of them fascinating. Every time I fear I have run out of subjects to write about, I discover something new and noteworthy about this community's past—such as the woman who became one of Connecticut's first female physicians, despite having an abusive, drunken father; the man who orchestrated a helicopter evacuation of more than one thousand Americans from Saigon just before the city fell to the North Vietnamese; or the Pulitzer Prize–winning historian who found Ridgefield, as a place to walk, more beautiful than a Burgundian village. A woman who built one of the town's most beautiful homes went on to build one of Manhattan's landmark skyscraper hotels. Her neighbor was an unsung pioneer in the world of vertical takeoff aircraft. And from the ridge on which they both lived, a boy who would later help Nathaniel Hawthorne get published would set out before dawn to hunt passenger pigeons a century earlier.

These are just a few of the tales of "hidden history" offered in these pages, a sort of sequel to *Ridgefield Chronicles*, published in 2014. They relate little-known pieces of what makes Ridgefield a remarkable place to live, work, visit—or write history. I hope you enjoy these accounts.

1

Places of the Past

We're an Original

"Ridgefield" is one of those nice, straightforward, combination names that the English settlers so often applied to New England places. It is an original name, not a copy of a location elsewhere, and was probably dreamed up by one of the two dozen pioneers who purchased the new territory from the American Indians in 1708.

As far as we can tell, Ridgefield was not named for any earlier locality; there is no "Ridgefield" in England, the source of many New England town names. In fact, it is quite likely that Ridgefield represented the first application of that name to a town, although there are at least four other Ridgefields in the United States today.

The name follows the same method used to come up with place names like Springfield, Longmeadow, Deerfield, Stockbridge, Brookfield, Northfield, Norwood and Medfield, all found in Massachusetts. They represent descriptions of the territory, whether it be terrain (Brookfield), wildlife (Deerfield) or location (Norwood or "north wood").

The inspiration for the name is easy to imagine. The new territory was largely lofty land. Moreover, the proprietors—the first landowners—selected one of the highest ridges for the central settlement. In fact, studies have indicated that the village of Ridgefield has the highest elevation—up to eight hundred feet above sea level—of any settled village along the entire East Coast of the United States. I'm not sure how far from the sea one can go in search of a higher village, but it can be reasonably said that Ridgefield is pretty high up for this part of the country, especially for a place from which you can see the sea (as you still can in a few parts of town).

The American Indian word for the village area also reflected this elevation; *caudatowa* was said to mean "high place."

New England villages were frequently situated on ridges. In his book *Norwood; or, Village Life in New England* (1886), Henry Ward Beecher—who had preached in Ridgefield several times—mused over this:

> *Did the New England settler alight upon hill-tops like a sentinel, or a hawk up the topmost bough, to spy danger at its first appearing? Or had he some unconscious sense of the poetic beauty of the scriptural city set upon a hill—some Jerusalem, lifted up, and seen from afar in all its beauty? Or was he willing to face the sturdy winds of New England hill-tops rather than to take the risk of malaria in the softer air of her valleys?*
>
> *Whatever the reason, the chosen spot in the early days seems to have been a high and broad backed hill, where the summer came last and departed earliest; where, while it lingered, it was purest and sweetest; where winter was most austere, and its winds roared among the trees and shook the framed houses with such awful grandeur, that children needed nothing more to awaken in their imagination the great Coming Judgment, and the final consuming storms when the earth should be shaken and should pass away.*

Of course, when the name was dreamed up, few "fields" lay here, the surface of the land being covered chiefly with trees. However, the proprietors no doubt envisioned thousands of acres of tilled fields where so many trees then stood. In fact, they called the new settlement a "plantation," a word that had been used to describe earlier Connecticut settlements, such as Norwalk.

"We find it to be accomodated with upland considerbly good & for quantity sufficient for thirty families, or more, and as for meedow & and meedow Land something [more or less] surpassing [both for quantity as well as quality] what is comon to be found in many larger plantations," wrote John Copp and John Raymond after surveying the Indian lands of Ridgefield in 1708 for a report to the colonial legislature.

In 1709, that legislature granted permission for the creation of a new town and, in so acting, first used the name of "Ridgfield." That spelling appeared on colony maps into the 1760s. However, "Ridgefield" soon took over as the preferred spelling locally.

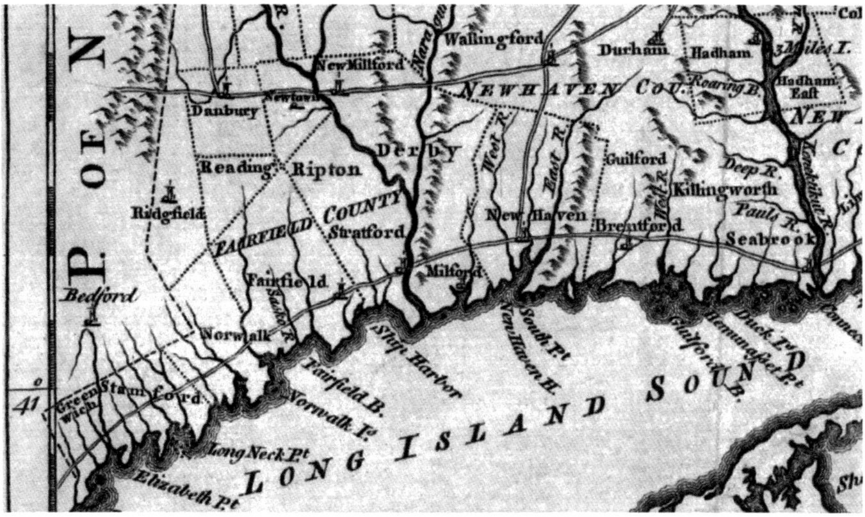

While Ridgefield was at first spelled Ridgfield, townspeople were soon writing it as Ridgefield. Maps, however, took a while to catch up. This is from Thomas Kitchin's 1758 map of Connecticut (which has New Milford incorrectly placed to the upper right of Ridgefield). *Library of Congress.*

Of the four other Ridgefields in Washington, Illinois, New Jersey and Ohio, at least two are probably named after our town.

Ridgefield, Ohio, is a township near such other Ohio localities as Norwalk, Lyme, Groton, Hartford, Norwich, Oxford and Sherman, all Connecticut town names as well. These communities are in what was called the Firelands, a territory that was once part of the Western Reserve, given to Connecticut residents whose houses were burned by the British during the Revolution. (Ridgefield people claimed sixty-five losses worth £1,736.) The huge territory granted to the state in compensation was on and south of Lake Erie, between Cleveland and Toledo.

Ridgefield, Washington, was definitely named for our town. The small community near the Oregon border was founded by Reverend Aaron L. Lindsley, a Presbyterian clergyman who had served from 1852 to 1868 as minister of the South Salem Presbyterian Church in neighboring Lewisboro, New York. He then went to Oregon, founding missions and churches there.

"When the little missionary community in the wilderness of Clarke County along the Columbia River was established, Dr. Lindsley's two sons, George and Addison, were among the original settlers," wrote Ridgefield historian Silvio Bedini. "When a name for the community was being selected, it was their suggestion that it be called Ridgefield in memory of the pleasant little town in Connecticut which they remembered from their childhood."

In 1953, when the dial telephone system was finally installed in Ridgefield, Washington, the first call made over the new equipment was to Ridgefield, Connecticut, for an exchange of greetings.

CHICKEN AND HIS ROCK

When the settlers began building the town in 1708 or so, they weren't the only newcomers. A number of American Indians had only recently arrived in the neighborhood. Chicken's Rock, a large outcropping alongside the Martin Park bathing beach at Great Pond, recalls these Indians' leader: Chicken or Chickens Warrups, one of the territory's most colorful characters. "A large rock on the shores of Great Pond...is still called Chickens' Rock, as it was a favorite spot where the old warrior used to sit," Ridgefield historian George L. Rockwell wrote in 1927.

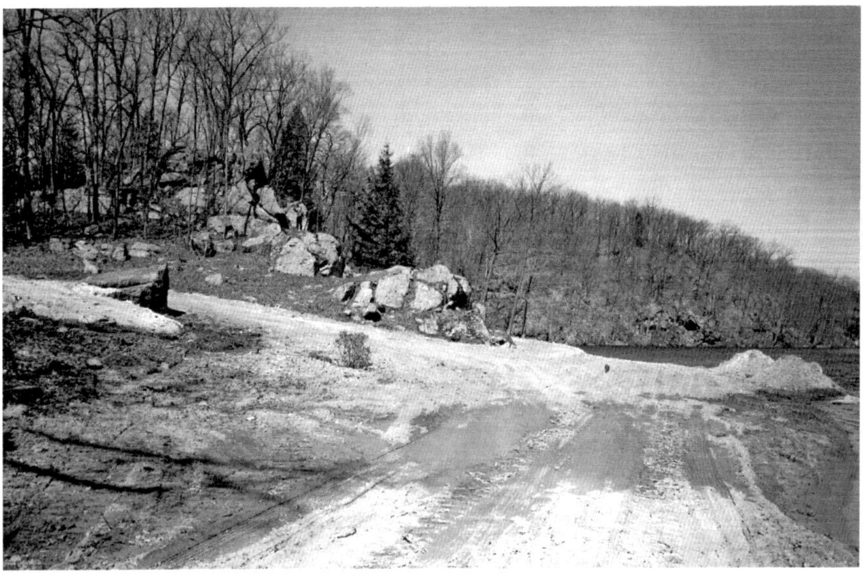

Chicken's Rock is shown in 1963 as work was underway to extend the Great Pond beach, now Martin Park, to reach the rock area. *Clarence Korker photograph,* Ridgefield Press *archives.*

In his *History of Fairfield County* (1881), D. Hamilton Hurd said:

> [A] *tract of land embraced within the bounds of the present town of Redding was claimed by a small and unimportant tribe of Indians, composed of a few stragglers or disaffected members of the Potatucks of Newtown, the Paugusetts of Milford, and the Mohawks of New York. This motley tribe was presided over by a chief bearing the euphonious name of Chicken Warrups, or Sam Mohawk, as he was sometimes called. It is supposed that he was a sagamore or under-chief of the powerful Mohawks, one of the tribes of the celebrated league of the Iroquois which inhabited New York, and who for some reason fled from his tribe and settled on Greenfield Hill. Here he killed an Indian and fled to Redding. He was a shrewd, cunning and important character in the early history of the town* [of Fairfield, then including Redding].

Researcher Franklyn Bearce, who considered himself a descendant of Chicken Warrups, maintains that this account of a murder in Fairfield is incorrect and tells a more colorful tale of homicide: "In his youth Chicken first killed an Onandaga youth of nonroyal blood over a girl, and the Grand Council banished him from the Five Nations; had he not been of noble Iroquois blood, he would have paid [for] the murder with his life. After he was banished and took the trail, he drifted into Connecticut, and…was captured by the Ramapoos, and his life was saved when the daughter [of] Catoonah claimed him for a husband." That's the same Catoonah, or Katonah, who was the Indian leader who sold the Ridgefield settlers their first twenty thousand acres in 1708.

In 1714, Chicken Warrups sold a sizable piece of land in the Lonetown area of Redding, then part of Fairfield, to John Read, an attorney after whom Reading, later Redding, was named. Warrups subsequently sold other tracts to the settlers, but in a 1725 deed, he reserved "liberty for myself and my heirs to hunt, fish, and fowl upon the land and in the waters, and further reserving for myself, my children, and grandchildren and their posterity the use of so much land by my present dwelling house or wigwam as…necessary for my or their personal improvement, that is to say, my children, children's children and posterity."

Over the years, however, Warrups battled with the colonists over details of the agreements he'd signed, and on several occasions, he petitioned Connecticut's colonial leaders to clear up his problems. In *The History of Redding, Connecticut*, Charles Burr Todd says the chief "seems to have been a strange mixture of

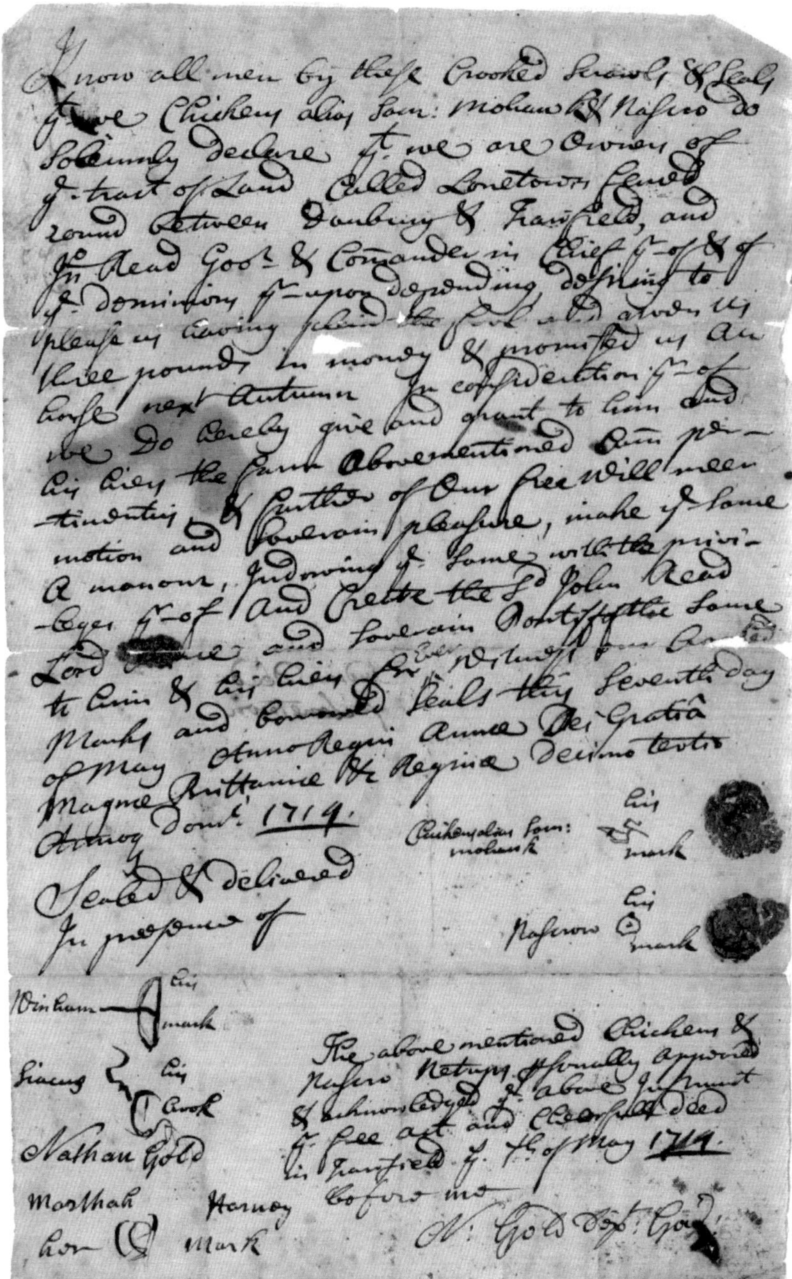

The 1714 deed in which Chicken Warrups and Naseco, another Indian, sold John Read the Lonetown section of Redding. "His mark" appears to the left of the top seal, where he is identified as Chickens, alias Sam Mohawk. *Courtesy of the Redding Historical Society.*

Indian shrewdness, rascality and cunning, and was in continual difficulties with the settlers concerning the deeds which he gave them."

Warrups also provoked some fear. In 1720, according to colonial records, there was a rumor that he had "lately received two belts of wampumpeag from certain remote Indians—as it is said, to the west of Hudson River—with a message expressing their desire to come and live in this colony." That rumor sparked "considerable apprehensions of danger from Indians, fearing that the belts have been sent on some bad design"—namely, plans to invade the "frontier towns" like Redding and Ridgefield. The governor and the colony council ordered a meeting with Warrups about the "threat," and while Todd found no official record of what happened, we can assume that no Indian invasion occurred or probably was ever contemplated by the natives themselves.

Any concerns about Chicken Warrups came to an end in 1749, when the chief took John Read's offer of two hundred acres near the Schaghticoke Reservation along the Housatonic River in Kent, giving up any rights to his old lands in Redding. It is said Warrups found the fishing and hunting better in Kent. He died about 1765. He was survived by a son, Tom Warrups, who had served with the American forces in the Revolutionary War, enlisting from Redding.

The Warrups family continued to create concerns in Redding long after Chicken's death. In 1815, Redding selectmen noted in their minutes, "Eunice Warrups, an Indian woman, was born in this town, is upwards of 70 years old; has been absent 50 years; came from New Milford, she says, 1st day of Nov; came to this town; was warned to depart." Towns back then were finicky about whom they admitted. They feared indigents; under law, once indigents had established themselves in a community, the selectmen could become responsible for their welfare. Hence, the tight-fisted officials in towns like Redding and Ridgefield often ordered indigents to leave before they could become welfare cases. Eunice might have been a daughter or granddaughter of Tom Warrups, the Revolutionary veteran. If so, one would have thought she'd have been treated better.

While Chicken's Rock is in Ridgefield within an arrow's shot of Redding, the land on which it sits—a small wedge that projected into Ridgefield as part of Governor Fitch's Farm (a 120-acre tract that spread across both towns)—was once considered Redding's. As a result of a 1786 petition to the General Assembly, this wedge—and the rock—became Ridgefield territory.

Incidentally, in the eastern side of the town of Westport (also once part of Fairfield) lies Machamux Park, a small open space between Green's Farms Road and I-95 near the Beachside Avenue curve. A plaque on a large boulder in the park reports, "The name according to legend means 'the beautiful land' and was named by Chickens, a young sachem who settled here."

THE SETTLERS AND THEIR ROCK

The settlers had their own rock, but they didn't use it for contemplation.

In the late 1600s, Norwalk residents were investigating the possibility of acquiring the American Indian lands above the northern boundary of their town—now the Wilton-Ridgefield line—and southerly of the recently settled town of Danbury. By the standards of those days, Norwalk had become "crowded." Most of Norwalk had been divided up for farm, pasture and woodlands, and the population of Norwalk, founded in 1653 as a plantation, was growing.

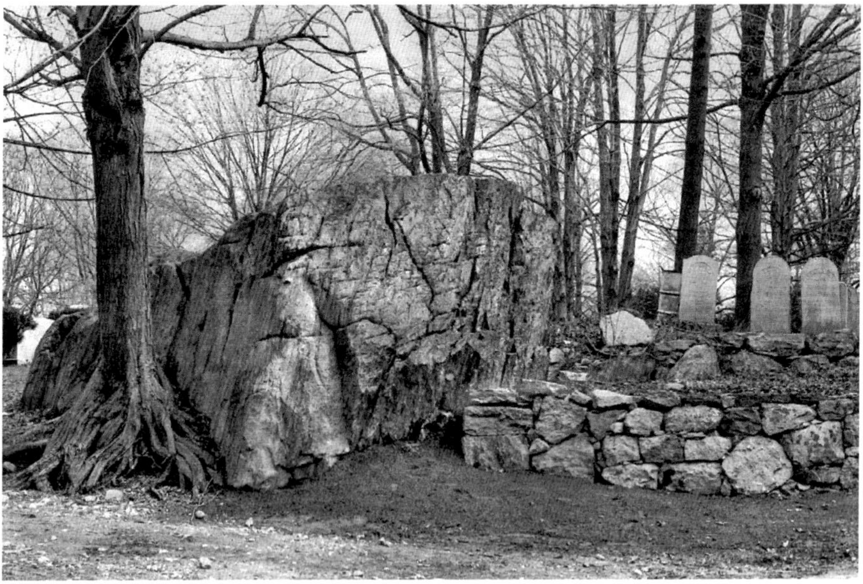

Settlers Rock is on North Salem Road adjoining the cemeteries. Some of the founders of the town are said to have spent their first night here atop the rock, surrounded by fires to keep wolves and wildcats away. *From the* Ridgefield Press *archives.*

In 1697, a group of Norwalk men was appointed to walk the Indian territory to see if the land was good for farming and if the water supply was adequate for mills. Both good land and decent water power would be needed for a new settlement. It is not clear what happened at that point, but it wasn't until 1706 that John Copp was appointed to "view" the land. Copp, who eventually laid out the design of Main Street and its home lots, was satisfied

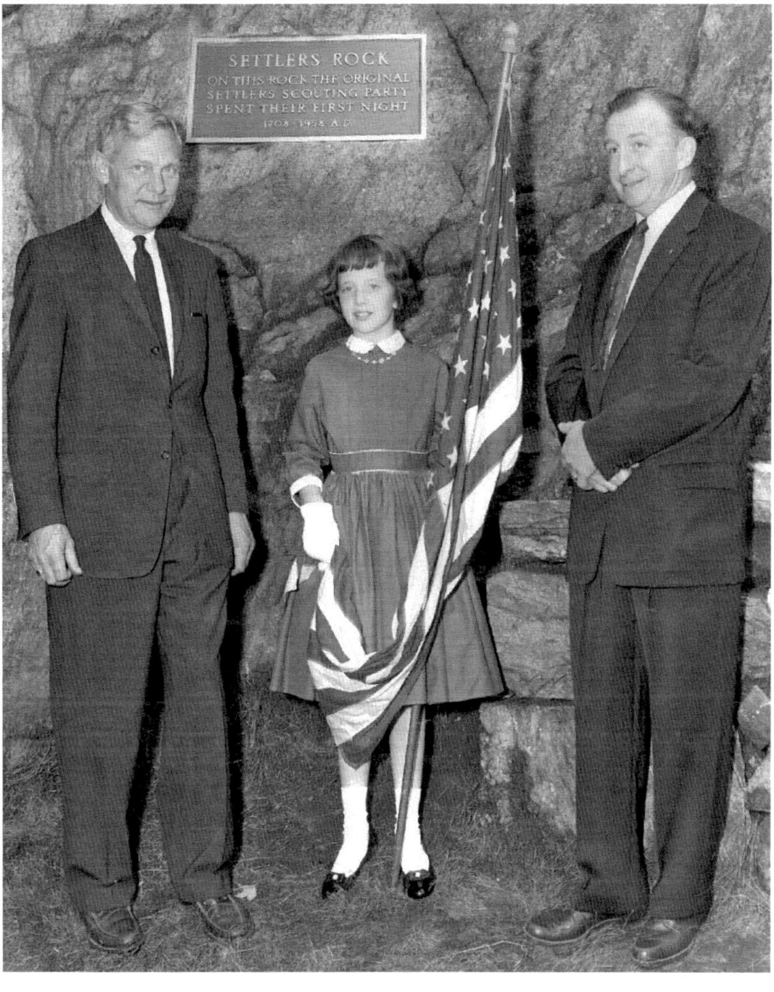

In 1958, a plaque noting the significance of Settlers Rock was erected during the town's 250th anniversary. From left are *Ridgefield Press* publisher Karl S. Nash, flag carrier Mary "Moo Moo" Venus and her father, Postmaster Richard E. Venus. The two men were among the organizers of the "semiquincentennial." *From the* Ridgefield Press *archives.*

that the territory was good, and in 1708, Norwalk residents petitioned the colony government to create a new town.

Legend says that when the time neared to move up from Norwalk into the new territory, five of the first settlers scouted the future village and spent their first night atop the large rock situated along North Salem Road at the Ridgefield Cemetery, nearly opposite New Street. It became known as Settlers Rock.

"The howling of wolves and the cry of the wild-cat filled them with terror, and one can imagine that daylight was greeted with much joy," speculated historian George L. Rockwell. Silvio Bedini, another Ridgefield historian, said, "They built fires around the base of the great boulder to protect them against wild animals." The descriptions present an eerie image of a handful of men huddled atop a giant boulder with flames encircling its base.

There is no contemporary written record of all this, but Bedini also speculates that even before the arrival of the proprietors, Settlers Rock would have been well known to explorers and may have sheltered John Copp and others who ventured into the territory on surveying or perhaps hunting missions. The rock was near the center of the first purchase of Indian lands, was along an Indian path and was large enough to have stood out as a landmark.

In 1958, during the town's 250th anniversary celebration, a plaque was mounted on the rock, stating, "On this rock the original settlers' scouting party spent their first night." The shape of the rock served as the logo for that 250th celebration.

BAILEY'S LIVELY LIFE

While hardly among the oldest or longest roads in town, Bailey Avenue has one of the most colorful histories, especially for a road of its size. Today, it's the home of shops, restaurants, homes, offices and a municipal parking lot; it also serves as a short cut to avoid Main Street traffic. But yesterday, it was more residential and loaded with life—and a little tragedy.

The doglegged road between Main Street and Prospect Street was named for Lewis H. Bailey, who developed it in the 1870s, soon after the railroad arrived in the village. Bailey, who lived from 1818 to 1899 and was the second president of the Ridgefield Savings Bank, felt the road would allow development of more businesses and homes and would serve as a shortcut

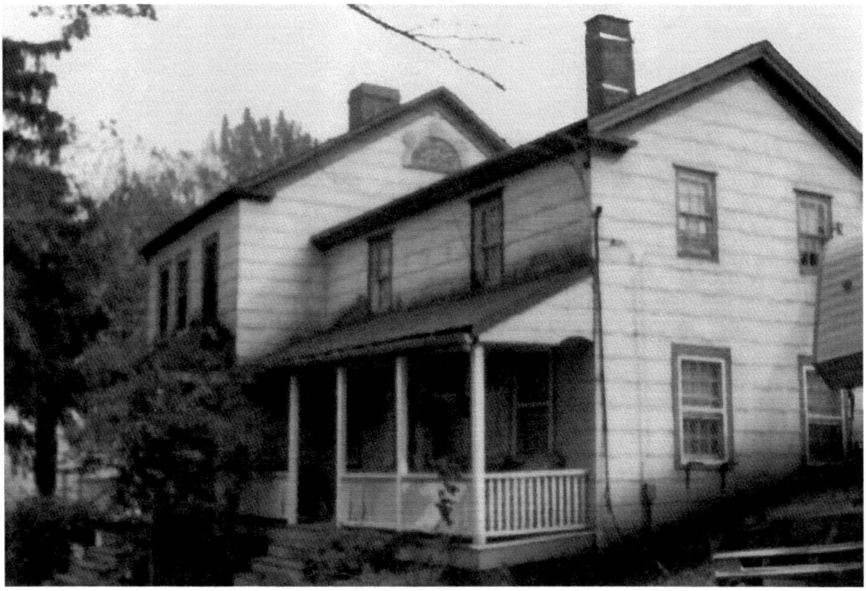

This house on Bailey Avenue, a speakeasy and dance hall in the 1920s, was originally two houses on Main Street that were moved here and joined in the late 1800s. It was razed to make way for offices. *Courtesy of the Ridgefield Historical Society.*

to the small freight yard along its eastern leg, where the branch railroad line ended. An old railroad warehouse still stands along the lower leg, used in modern times for shops, offices and storage.

In the early twentieth century, Bailey Avenue was home to many immigrant Italian families, the descendants of whom still lived there in the early twenty-first century.

Ann Lent Van Wagner, who was born on Bailey Avenue in 1896, had fond memories of life long ago along the road when she was interviewed in 1973.

Van Wagner lived across the street from a house that once stood on the south side, just as the road veers northward. That old house served as a center of entertainment during the 1920s. The Mei family had a speakeasy there and a small dance hall behind the house. "We used to dance every Saturday night," she said. Despite Prohibition, the Meis somehow obtained barrels of beer via freight car—the tracks from Branchville ended right next to the Mei house. Tony Mei used to serve drinks of all sorts through a small window in the dance hall. Mei insisted that customers behave themselves. One night, Van Wagner said, there was a drunken brawl at the hall. Angered at the mêlée, Mei grabbed some boards and nailed them across the serving window. "No more drink," he said, keeping the dance hall dry for a while as a lesson to the brawlers.

Ann Van Wagner recalled several large old buildings that stood on the south side, just east of the *Ridgefield Press* building, probably built by Bailey. Here many working-class families—both black and white—lived in apartments; Bailey Avenue, she said, was the most integrated road in town. The late Paul J. Morganti, a selectman and head of a multimillion-dollar international construction firm, was born in an apartment house there. Among the many colorful residents of Bailey Avenue early in the twentieth century was "Charlie Peanuts" (Charles Stannard), who owned a peanut cart and would sell his nuts and other snacks at the many baseball games and other outdoor events in town.

During Prohibition, bootleg wine and other alcoholic beverages sometimes arrived at lower Bailey Avenue by freight car. The state police—whose barracks were on nearby East Ridge—would periodically pull a raid, roll the barrels up to Main Street or along Bailey Avenue and smash them open with axes in the middle of the road for all to see. Many members of the Italian American community never forgot that and, long after, disliked the state police and certain of its leaders.

One such raid occurred in February 1926, offering what must have been a shocking and sad sight for local oenophiles. State police entered a house on Prospect Street and confiscated twenty barrels "of what is reported as being very good wine, some of it having been imported from Europe," the *Ridgefield Press* reported. Police poured the contents onto the snow and arrested the owners of the house. At the nearby store of Brunetti and Gasparini at Prospect and Bailey Avenue, twenty cases of beer and other alcoholic beverages were confiscated.

Bailey Avenue has seen plenty of excitement of the incendiary kind. On November 22, 1906, an arsonist set fire to Hiram K. Scott Jr.'s large livery stable—which had survived the Great Fire of 1895 that destroyed all the buildings to the west. Scott rebuilt, but his one-story brick building soon served automobiles instead of horses. The garage later became the offices and printing plant of the *Ridgefield Press* (which added a second story in 1975).

A year after the Scott fire, S.D. Keeler's grain elevator at the railroad warehouses was heavily damaged by fire.

Between Scott's Garage and the town hall stood Coleman's Lunch Café. In December 1921, a gasoline stove exploded, severely burning Ben Brown, a cook, and destroying the small restaurant. Owner Michael Coleman rebuilt the place, which continued to operate into the 1930s.

On April 22, 1922, a tenement on Bailey Avenue caught fire and burned to the ground, igniting other buildings, including Bates' Garage, which was destroyed. The *Press* charged that the water company failed to keep its West Mountain standpipe full, leaving virtually no pressure to protect the buildings adjacent to the garage. The paper cited other fires where firefighters lacked water pressure.

The *Ridgefield Press* was the center of one of the more exciting days in recent Bailey Avenue history. On March 29, 1985, gasoline leaking from a service station's underground tank next door was sucked from the ground water by a sump pump in the cellar of the *Press* building and then emptied into the storm sewers. Down the road, gas fumes exploded, damaging a workshop in the old warehouse, and the fire department closed down the *Press* offices and the gas station for several days until all was safe.

The worst tragedy on Bailey Avenue involved fire in a different way. In March 1962, a defective space heater produced carbon monoxide that killed

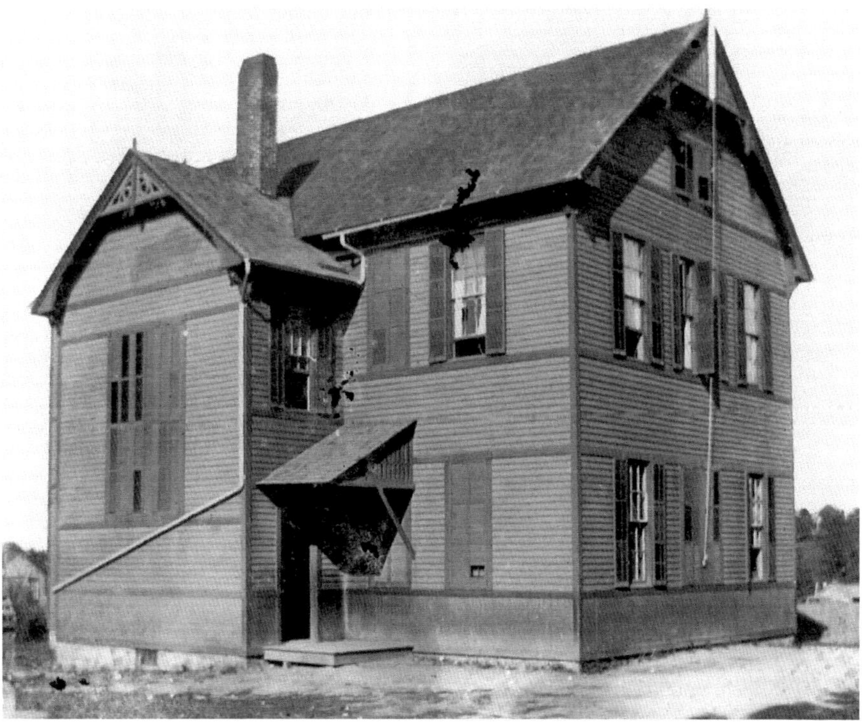

Over its long life, the Center/Garden School, shown here in the 1890s, served children from preschool to twelfth grade. Its site is now the Bailey Avenue parking lot. *From the* Ridgefield Press *archives.*

an eighty-six-year-old woman and her forty-five-year-old daughter in their Bailey Avenue apartment.

For many years, Bailey Avenue was also a center of education. The Center School was built there in the late 1800s, serving most of the village's pupils. When the new grammar school was completed on East Ridge in 1915, the Center School became Hamilton High School. Later, the high school moved to the expanded grammar school building, and the Bailey Avenue school then led a long existence as the Garden School, which served the town's youngest scholars. In 1955, when Veterans Park School opened nearby, the Garden School was torn down to make way for Ridgefield's first municipal parking lot. Back in 1955, many opposed the parking lot, saying that no one would walk all the way from there to the shops on Main Street. By the 1970s and 1980s, the lot had become so full of "walkers," as well as workers in shops and offices, that the town began planning more lots with the help of its new Parking Authority.

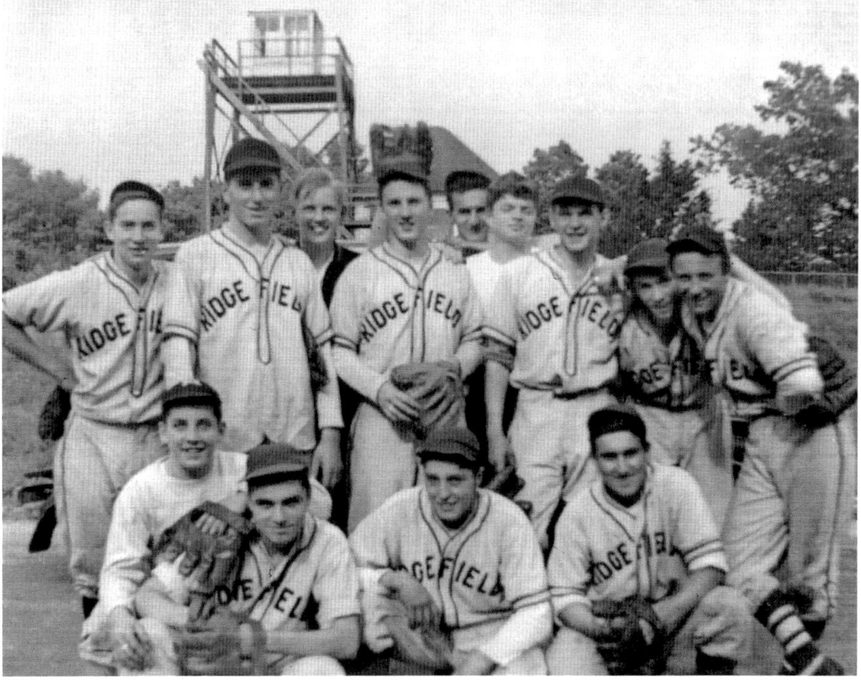

The 1946 Ridgefield High School baseball team poses for a team shot with the World War II airplane spotting tower and its octagonal office in the background (only the roof of the office is visible). The scene is behind the old high school. The office is now on Bailey Avenue. *Courtesy of the Ridgefield Historical Society.*

One of the more unusual structures on Bailey Avenue is a small round building, right on the curve next to the Casey Energy fuel depot, which is used as an office. The building was moved there many years ago from behind the old Ridgefield High School on East Ridge, where it had served as the office for an aircraft-spotting tower that was attached to it. Local volunteers used the tower to scan the skies for enemy planes during World War II and the Korean War. Fortunately, no enemies were ever spotted.

Bailey Avenue has the distinction of being the first one-way road in town, an arrangement approved by the Police Commission around 1973 to ease traffic congestion in the village. One of the problems had been the fact that Bailey Avenue isn't directly across from Catoonah Street along Main Street, leading to a jog that created traffic circulation headaches.

Although the road had been in use for more than a century, the town learned in the summer of 1976 that it had never obtained title to the end at Prospect Street. Technically speaking, the road was still privately owned. Using its attorneys and the cooperation of neighboring landowners, the town eventually acquired ownership.

AN OUTPOST FOR MAN AND TREE

Bennett's Pond State Park is one of Ridgefield's environmental treasures. Wild, hilly and more than four hundred acres, it seems like an unspoiled wilderness. One piece of the past, however, often surprises hikers as they reach the top of a prominent hill not far from the entrance to the park. There, amid wildflowers, wild berry bushes and old trees, is a patch of pavement.

That asphalt was once part of the courtyard at the end of the driveway to Outpost Farm, the mansion of Colonel Louis D. Conley, a man who once owned most of the northeast side of town. In its heyday, that courtyard served coaches and carriages arriving at the mansion, and later, it served as the entrance to a famous inn.

Outpost Farm's mansion was the center of a two-thousand-acre estate that included a dozen or more houses in which many members of the colonel's staff lived, a sizable farm with brick barns, a large kennel that raised champion dogs, an inn that drew the rich and famous and one of the largest nurseries in the Northeast. And while the house and most other Outpost buildings are gone today, the colonel's finest legacy—countless thousands of trees—remains.

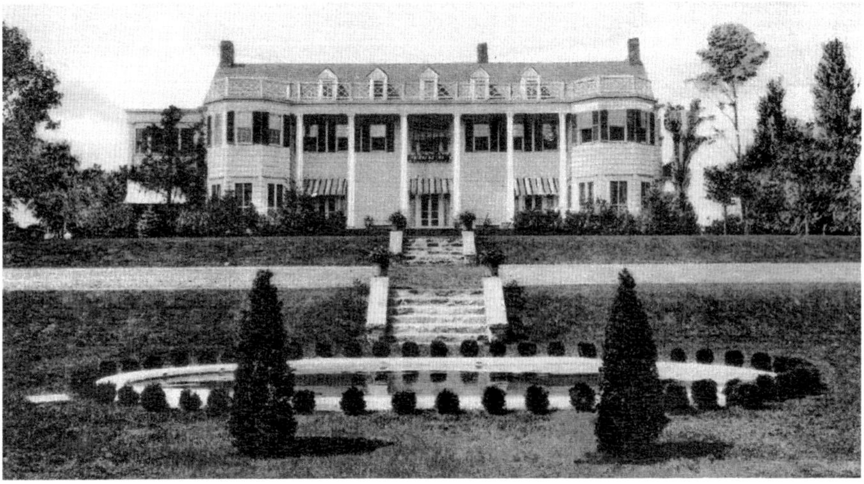

The mansion at Outpost Farm later became the Fox Hill Inn. This is the front of the house, with a decorative pool in the foreground. *Postcard from author's collection.*

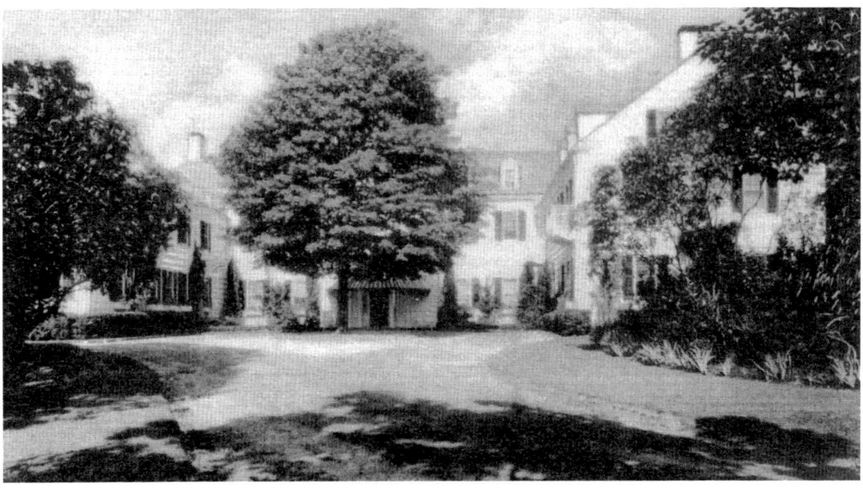

The courtyard of Outpost Farm, later the Fox Hill Inn, served arriving vehicles. The pavement is still there, as is that tree in the middle, now much larger. *Circa 1946 postcard from author's collection.*

Born in 1874, Louis Daniel Conley grew up in New York City and once commanded the New York National Guard's "Fighting 69th" Division. He and his two brothers ran a large tinfoil company, founded by their father. Around 1914, Colonel Conley bought an old farm on Bennett's Farm Road and began turning its fields and pastures into an "outpost" from New York

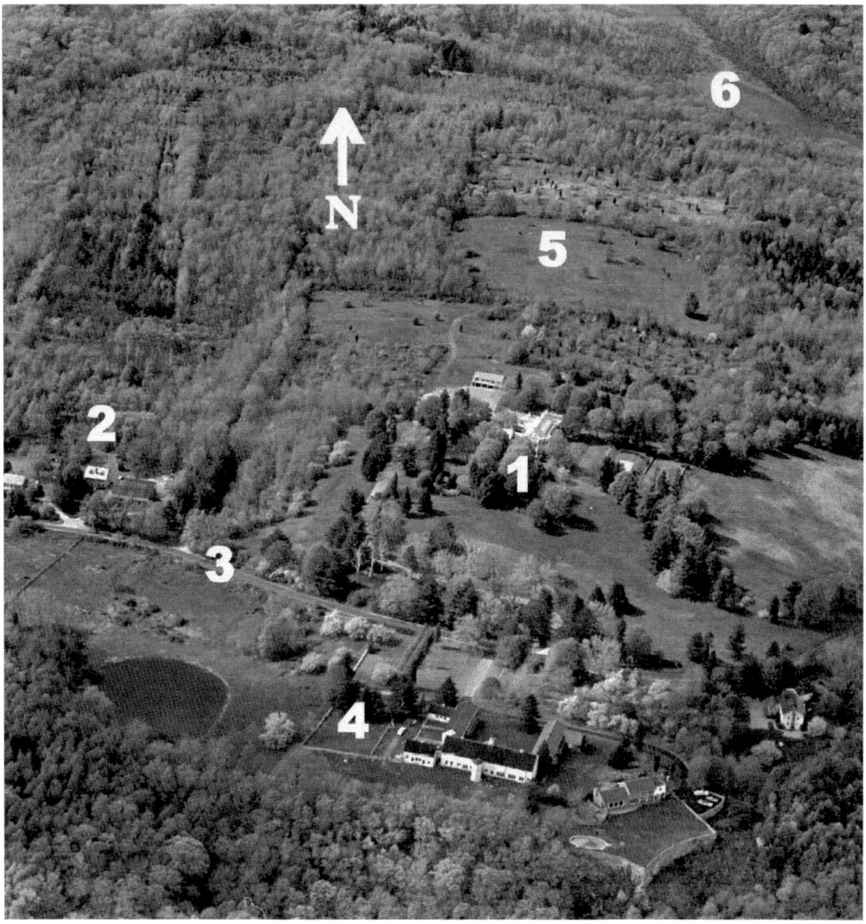

Outpost Farm in 1970, when the mansion was Fox Hill Inn. Everything north of the road is now Bennett's Pond State Park and mostly woods: 1. mansion; 2. staff houses (now park parking); 3. Bennett's Farm Road; 4. barns, staff houses, etc.; 5. field, still extant; 6. Bennett's Pond. *Jimmy Thalacker photograph, from the* Ridgefield Press *archives.*

City life and its summer heat. He eventually built a small, self-contained empire. Outpost Farm grew its own crops, raised livestock, maintained a water system with a ninety-thousand-gallon storage tank (which burned down in a spectacular 1974 arson) and produced its own electricity (the generator had two, 4,500-pound flywheels). He also established and operated a summer camp for poor city boys, complete with a swimming pool and a professional director, on his estate and was a major promoter of Boy Scouting in Connecticut.

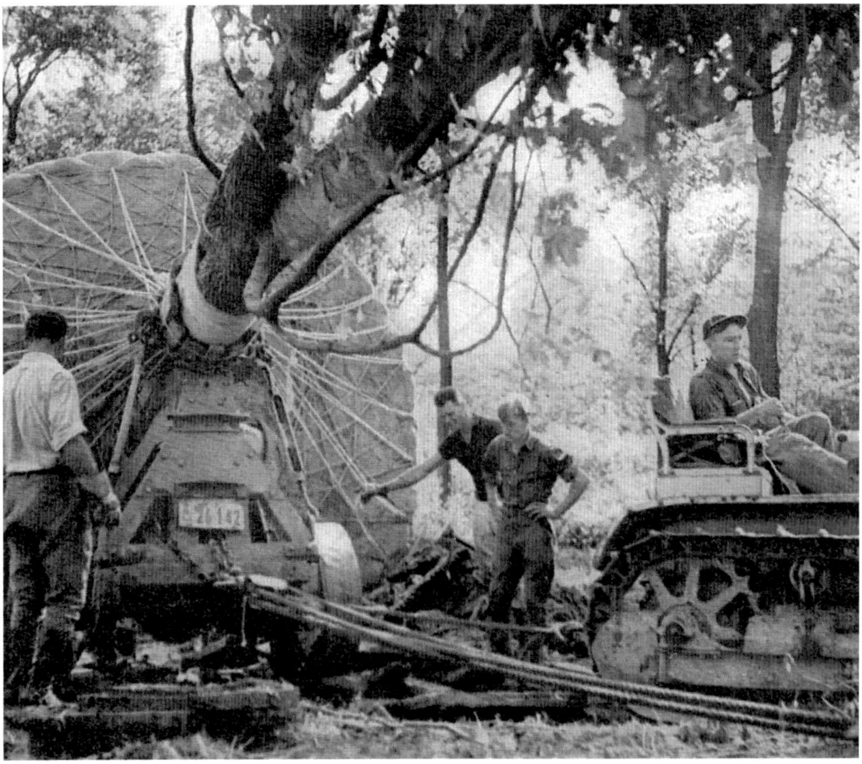

A 1930s Outpost Nurseries crew removes a sizable tree to haul to a client somewhere in the Northeast. *From an Outpost Nurseries catalogue in the archives of the* Ridgefield Press.

In 1923, Conley founded Outpost Nurseries and began buying many pieces of land; he eventually owned virtually every parcel along Route 35, Danbury Road, from today's Copps Hill area to Route 7 and almost all of the land along Route 7 from Farmingville into Danbury, plus most of the land between Routes 7 and 35. With his estate and his nursery, he held some two thousand acres—equal to nearly one-tenth the size of the town.

Outpost planted tens of thousands of trees and shrubs. Most were sold, but thousands still remain, nursery stock that has now grown wild into woodland. Many names of modern roads on the old nursery land reflect what was grown in the neighborhood: Copper Beech Lane, Poplar Road, Birch Lane, Linden Road, Cherry Lane, Dogwood Drive and Laurel Lane.

Among Outpost Nurseries' many jobs between 1925 and World War II were plantings for the 1933 Chicago World's Fair; the 1939 New York World's Fair; the National Art Gallery in Washington; many city parks;

Harvard, Yale and Williams College; and the estates of such people as Cole Porter, President Franklin D. Roosevelt and the Buckleys at Sharon. It also supplied the first official Rockefeller Center Christmas tree in 1933.

In 1930, the colonel opened the Outpost Inn on Danbury Road, converting an 1810 house and outbuildings into a restaurant and overnight accommodations that attracted many celebrities over the years; Eleanor Roosevelt dined there while her husband was president. The inn closed in the early 1960s, and the property was acquired by the Shapley School, a private prep school operated by Carl Shapley, son of the Harvard astronomer Harlow Shapley and brother of Nobel laureate economist Lloyd Shapley. The school lasted about four years before financial troubles forced its closing. In 1968, David L. Paul, who was building Casagmo on Main Street, acquired the property, calling it Fox Hill (after an inn that had operated in the colonel's house—see below). Fox Hill included the first condominiums ever built in Ridgefield; they were so successful that Paul converted all 286 units to condos and eventually did the same at the 320-unit Casagmo apartments. For many years, Outpost Pond on the inn property was a popular ice-skating spot in town; with the arrival of the condominiums, however, public skating ended.

Colonel Conley died in 1930, and the family operated Outpost Nurseries until 1945, when it became the much smaller Woodcock Nurseries, which lasted until the 1970s.

In 1946, Colonel Conley's thirty-four-room home became the Fox Hill Inn. Known for its fine dining and spectacular view of the countryside, the inn drew many diners from New York City. In 1970, owner John Yervant accepted an offer from IBM to sell the property. IBM wanted to use the site as a school for its executives in a country club setting. But IBM also wanted to be able to fly those executives in and out by helicopter, and the uproar over the potential aircraft noise prompted IBM to abandon its plans. Vandalized, decaying and a hazard, the Outpost/Fox Hill Inn mansion was torn down in 1975. IBM held on to the land until the 1990s, when it sold its holdings to a New Jersey developer called Eureka, which wanted to put multifamily housing there. After battling the developer for several years, the town acquired the Fox Hill Inn site and other former IBM land totaling 458 acres in 2001 and sold it to the state as a park two years later. (In 2015, Eureka still owned former Conley/IBM land on the south side of Bennett's Farm Road and still planned housing.)

One of the few remaining buildings in the Outpost empire is the former headquarters for the nurseries, located on Route 7 a little north of Route 35. The building has now been incorporated into the Stonehouse Commons condominiums there.

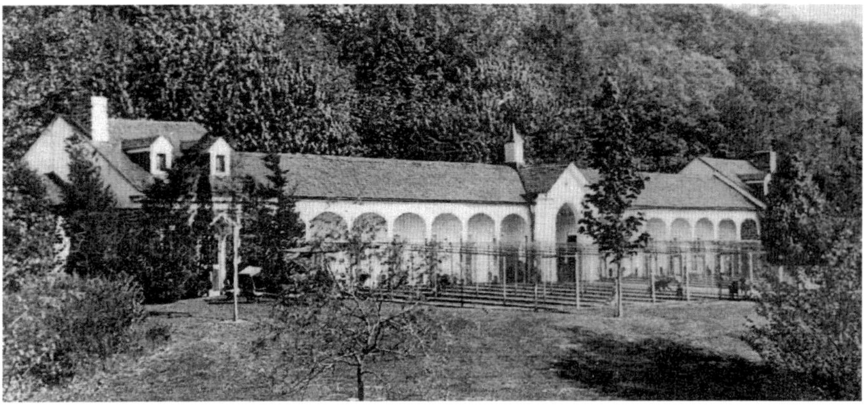

Colonel Louis D. Conley had as many as 140 terriers and spaniels in this kennel, once the largest in New England. It later became a research center, a steakhouse and an Italian restaurant. *Postcard from author's collection.*

Just to the south of this were the kennels where Colonel Conley raised his show dogs. The 175-foot-long building was said to have been the largest kennel in New England at the time. At one point, the colonel had twenty Kerry blue terriers (his favorite), nineteen Sealyham terriers, forty cocker spaniels and sixty English setters in the kennel. After the colonel's death, the building was acquired by Waldeck Kennels, which bred Saint Bernards and cocker spaniels. Later, the Coast Guard trained dogs there, and then the Gaines dog food company took it over as a research center. Finally, in the 1950s, the doghouse became a steakhouse and then, in the 1970s, the Red Lion. The Italian restaurant was torn down in 2006 to make way for the Terraces apartments.

When he died in 1930 of meningitis, Colonel Louis Conley was only fifty-six. In a front-page headline over his obituary, the *Ridgefield Press* called him "a man of large affairs." Indeed, thanks to the lands he amassed and the trees he planted, few people of the past have had such a large effect on the Ridgefield of today.

WHIPSTICK AND ITS ARTIST

Many people used to believe Whipstick Road got its name because Ridgefield's early disciplinarians would get their tools for public whippings from that part of town. Even George L. Rockwell, in his *History of Ridgefield*, maintained, "Whipstick District received its name from the whipping-post in colonial days. The whipping-post was on the [south] corner of Main Street and Branchville Road."

The story is quaint but probably apocryphal. For one thing, no corner of Branchville Road, which was built in the nineteenth century, existed when a whipping post might have stood on Main Street. What's more, Whipstick as a name was in use by 1712, before Ridgefield even had a minister, and it's unlikely there were enough sins—or sinners—to warrant having a whipping post so early on.

More probable is the theory of former first selectman Leo F. Carroll (1900–1985). Ridgefield's settlement occurred in the days of animal-centered transportation and farming power, and whipsticks were necessary devices for prodding horses, cattle and oxen. Carroll believed early farmers went to the Whipstick neighborhood to cut their sticks, perhaps because the kind of wood or sapling best suited for this purpose, such as holly, grew there. The name is one of the oldest in town still in use, so the characteristic of providing whipsticks must have been noteworthy then and long thereafter.

"Whipstick" was used in the eighteenth century mainly to apply to Whipstick Ridge, which runs along the east side of Nod Road from the Branchville Road area to the Wilton line. By the nineteenth century, the ridge was lending its name to the larger neighborhood, and deeds referring to land as simply "at Whipstick" began appearing.

Whipstick was a school district's name from as early as 1841. An 1865 deed refers to the "Whip-Stick School District"—maybe the deed's author used the dash to emphasize "whip" in a belief that the school was a prime employer of the stick to prod not animals but children into obedience. No doubt some strict masters and mistresses of the Whipstick schoolhouse used sticks from the district. Imagine what it must have been like for a nineteenth-century youngster attending a school named for this feared tool of corporal punishment!

The last Whipstick schoolhouse stood on the northern corner of Whipstick and Nod Roads. After it closed in 1915, the small building was incorporated into a wing of a stucco-covered house. Here, American painter and photographer Charles Sheeler lived and worked for ten years. Sheeler was one of the leading American artists of the twentieth century, famed for his precisionist paintings. As a photographer, he worked alongside Edward Steichen of Redding, was hired by Henry Ford to photograph his factories and worked for many years for such Conde Nast publications as *Vogue*.

Born in 1883 in Philadelphia, Sheeler studied art in France and was already a successful painter early in the twentieth century. But to help his

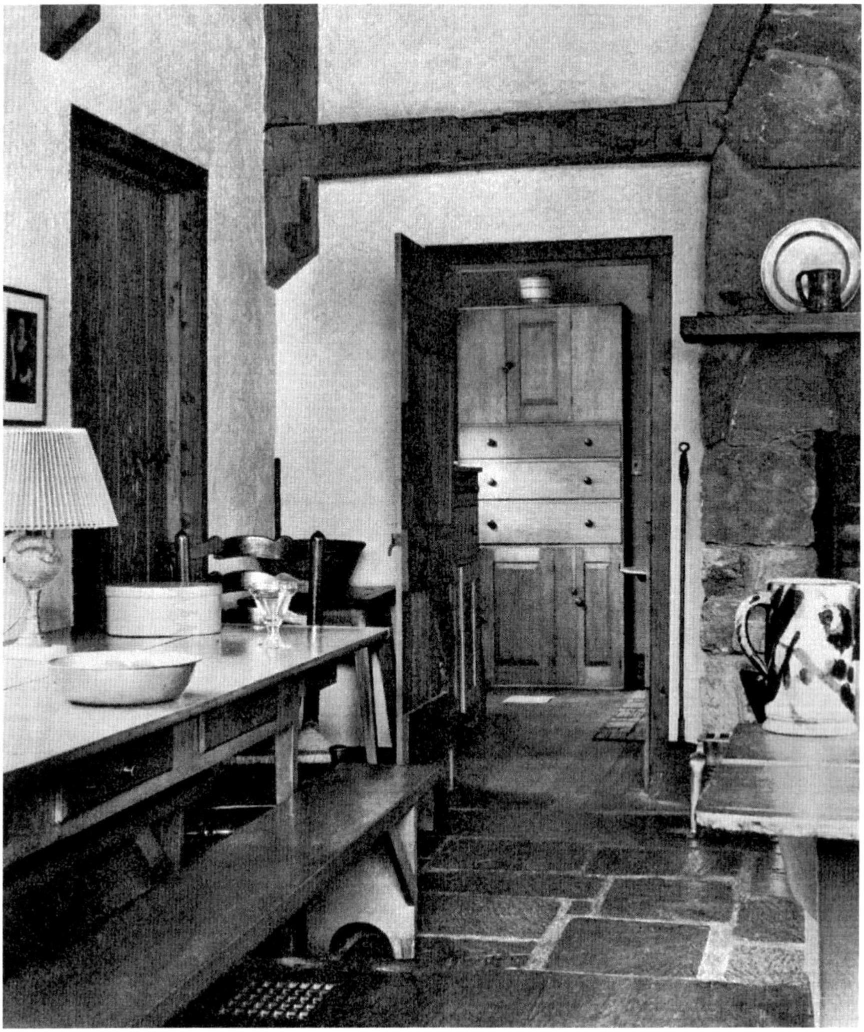

Charles Sheeler took this photograph, showing several examples of Shaker furniture, of his house in Ridgefield from his painting studio. It appears in the book *Charles Sheeler*, published by the Museum of Modern Art in 1939. *Digital Image © The Museum of Modern Art/Licensed by SCALA / Art Resource, New York.*

income, he turned to photography. That medium influenced his art, and his paintings took on the precision of a photograph. His work for Ford also influenced him, and he became best known as a painter of machines and industrial scenes as well as ships. His work is in many of the major museums, including the Museum of Modern Art and the Metropolitan Museum of Art.

Sheeler moved to the Whipstick house in 1932. He first wife died a year later. He married again in 1942 and moved to Irvington-on-Hudson, New York. He died in 1965.

Alas, his home here, schoolhouse and all, was torn down in 2000 to make way for a much larger house.

A HOUSE OF HISTORY AND FRIENDS

Another house with a lot of history was torn down in 2014, but little of its former glory was left by then. The large Victorian on Governor Street was razed to make way for the new Ridgefield Visiting Nurse Association headquarters. It was a building that had led four lives in its long history, during which it had housed a number of notable Ridgefielders.

The building originally stood on Main Street, in front of today's Community Center. Its birth date is unknown, but the structure existed in some form by 1850, when it was the home and office of Dr. Nehemiah Perry Sr. He was the son of Ridgefield's first physician, Dr. David Perry

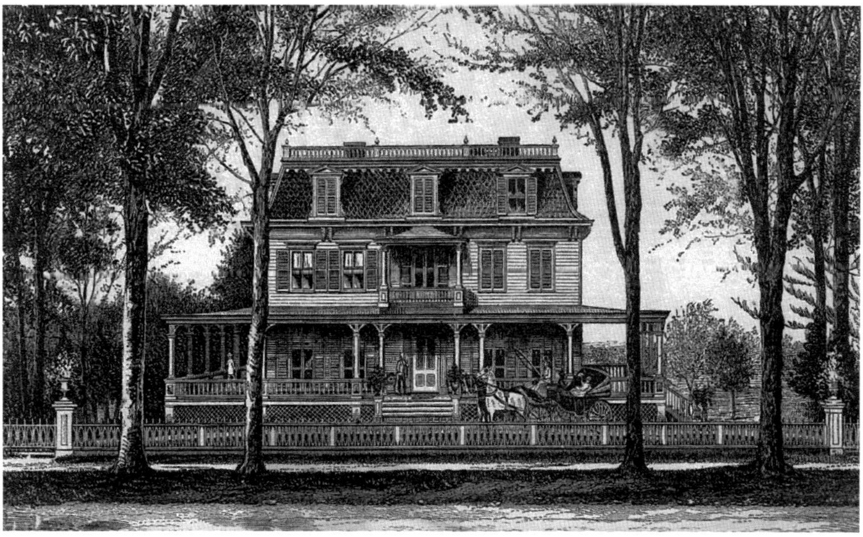

Governor Phineas Lounsbury's first home on Main Street is depicted in the 1878 *History of Ridgefield* by Reverend Daniel W. Teller. The Empire-style house, apparently originally Colonial style, had belonged to a family of prominent Ridgefield physicians. *From the author's collection.*

(1747–1822), a Yale graduate who came to town in 1772. David Perry was also an early rector of St. Stephen's Church, located directly across Main Street from the home site, and it's possible that the minister-physician had acquired the property, and perhaps the house, at some point in his career here. Maybe he had it built.

Based on census information, his son, Dr. Nehemiah Perry Sr., and his grandson, Nehemiah Jr., were both living in and practicing from the house by 1850. After Perry Sr. died in 1866, Perry Jr. decided he could not live in a house that held so many memories of family, so he sold it and moved south on Main Street. When Nehemiah Perry Jr. retired in 1893, it brought to an end 121 years of medical service to Ridgefield by three generations of one family.

The old house was sold to Judson Hawley and, a few years later, to Governor Phineas Lounsbury, who did quite a bit of gussying up, turning what had probably been a plain Colonial into an ornate Empire-style Victorian. In his 1878 book *The History of Ridgefield, Conn.*, Reverend Daniel W. Teller observes, "Mr. P.C. Lounsbury, having purchased the property best known as the 'Dr. Perry Place,' has made many marked and modern improvements about the house and grounds—improvements which are still going on and which, when completed, will make his residence second to none in the town." Teller was so impressed with the house that a picture of it was prominently placed near the beginning of his book (see page 33).

Born in 1844 on a farm in the Farmingville section of town, Phineas Chapman Lounsbury graduated from Wesleyan University, served in the Civil War and was a businessman in New York City, acting as chairman of the board of Atlantic National Bank and on the board of many other companies, including Ridgefield's First National Bank. He was also a partner in the family shoe factory in Norwalk. He began his political career in 1874 when he was elected a state representative from town. He became governor in 1887, elected to one two-year term.

Perhaps feeling that his house did not well serve a wealthy former governor of the state, Lounsbury decided in the 1890s that he needed a new, more stately home. Impressed by Connecticut's exhibition building at the 1893 Columbian Exposition in Chicago, he had a new house designed to imitate that building—it is today's Community Center, also called the Lounsbury Mansion.

In those days, people were less likely to tear down an old building, and like many other Main Street houses, the "Dr. Perry Place" was moved elsewhere—in this case, down the hill on Governor Street, where it was placed on a lot across the road from the governor's estate.

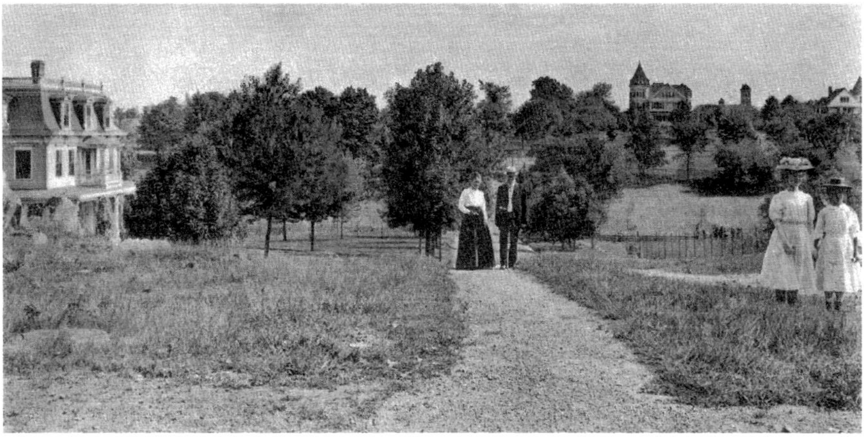

Governor Lounsbury's former home, later called the "House of Friends," is shown at left, circa 1905, with what appears to be a family on the sidewalk along Governor Street. In the background is an old Rockwell home that became the state police barracks and is today's Ridgefield Police headquarters. *From the author's collection.*

Here it became the home of Mary H. "May" Rockwell, daughter John W. Rockwell, longtime owner of the Elms Inn. She or her parents probably paid a modest price because the Rockwells and Lounsburys were relatives. The house was rather large for a single woman, so it wasn't long before Miss Rockwell began renting rooms in a boardinghouse fashion. She didn't rent to just anyone, however; she sought guests who were intellectually interesting as well as congenial, and she called the place the "House of Friends."

Among those friends, best known was Mabel Cleves, her companion of more than forty years. Cleves was a Columbia-educated daughter of an aristocratic Georgia family who came to town in 1898 to teach. The Montessori-trained instructor changed education in Ridgefield. She established not only the first kindergarten here but also a public preschool—some say the first in the nation—and helped get the town to modernize its schools in general. She also founded the PTA.

"She had a remarkable gift for teaching very young children, and she truly can be called 'a legend in her own time,'" wrote the late John White in 1990.

But Cleves did more than teach her kids over her forty-year career. "She had a permanent arrangement with Ryan's Country Store [on Main Street] to buy shoes or clothing for needy children in her classes," White said. "There were many poor students in her class. She always shared her meager salary in this way."

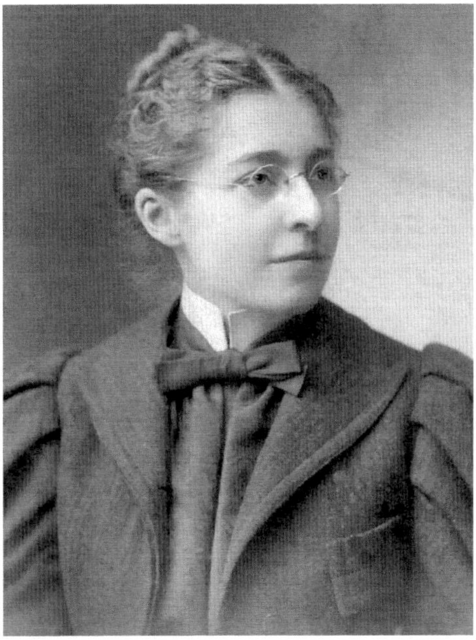

Left: Mary "May" Rockwell was the landlord of the House of Friends, which attracted artists and intellectuals. *Joseph Hartmann photograph, from the* Ridgefield Press *archives.*

Below: When he built his new mansion, Governor Lounsbury moved his former home to Governor Street, where it was eventually converted to offices. In 2014, it was torn down to make way for the new Ridgefield Visiting Nurse Association headquarters. *Photograph by Steve Coulter, the* Ridgefield Press.

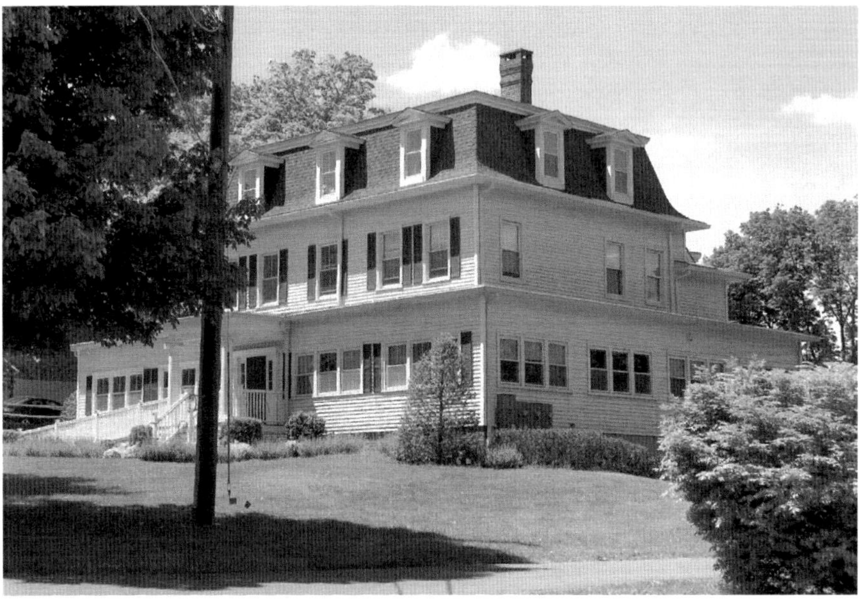

May Rockwell was an accomplished pianist who had studied at Centenary College and at Oberlin. She taught piano to hundreds of Ridgefield children over two decades, at first with her cousin Faustina

Hurlbutt. The Hurlbutt-Rockwell School of Music regularly gave public recitals at the House of Friends.

Besides long-term clientele, guests at the house included actors and actresses doing summer theater (see page 99), and teachers and professors on summer break. The place had a "high cultural level," the *Ridgefield Press* once reported. May Rockwell was "a great and wonderful woman," added White, a St. Luke's School teacher who was the last living alumnus of the House of Friends.

Frail and infirm, May Rockwell sold the house in 1947 and died two years later in a nursing home. Mabel Cleves died in 1952 and is remembered today in the name Cleves Auditorium at Veterans Park School.

Judge Joseph H. Donnelly (1906–1992) soon acquired the building. The business district in the 1950s was expanding, and Donnelly—who owned the adjacent land that's now a shopping center belonging to his family—decided to convert the place to offices. Over the years, most of the "many marked and modern improvements" that made the place "second to none in the town" were lost as the building was reworked several times to accommodate the needs of commercial offices, modern building and fire codes. So despite its long life of housing leading people in Ridgefield's history, little fuss was made about its being torn down for a new RVNA headquarters.

ELEVEN LEVELS LORE

The mansion at Eleven Levels, a West Mountain estate, has fared far better than the House of Friends and is still a home a century after it was built. Now a subdivision, the Eleven Levels estate may have gotten its name from the number of degrees of elevation that ripple through the property as it rolls down the eastern slope of West Mountain. However, "eleven" may have been chosen for a less numerical reason: its mellifluence with the word "levels."

The property was amassed and named by Arthur C. Fraser, a prominent New York City attorney who began in 1907 by buying 31 acres. By the time of his death in 1934, he had acquired fourteen parcels totaling 180 acres and extending all the way between West Mountain Road and Barrack Hill Road. When his estate was appraised in 1936, the value of the entire 180 acres was placed at $8,958. Today, a single acre there might fetch more than forty times that sum.

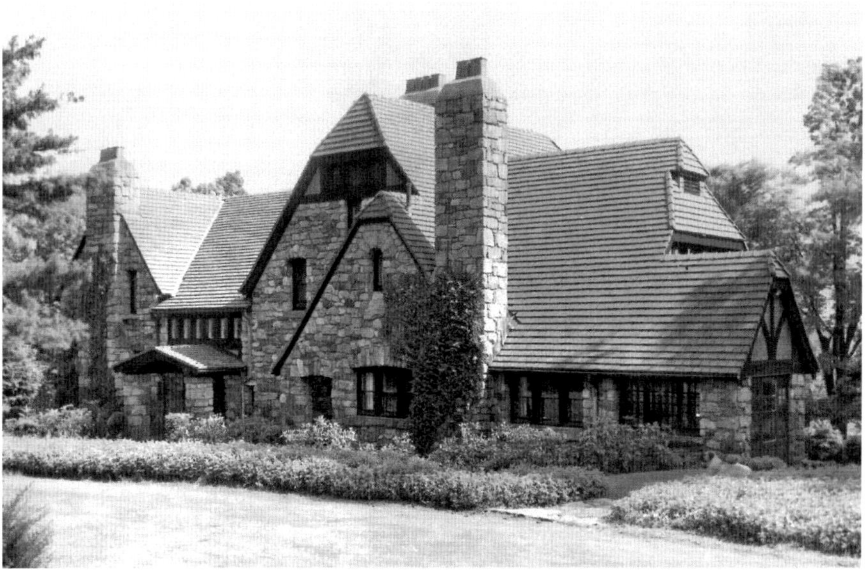

The mansion at Eleven Levels was designed by Grosvenor Atterbury and John A. Tompkins, who specialized in "weekend homes of the wealthy." *Courtesy of Ridgefield Historical Society.*

Described in his *Ridgefield Press* obituary as one of the best patent attorneys in the United States, Fraser was also a prominent figure in the New York City arts world and was benefactor of agencies helping the poor.

Grosvenor Atterbury and John A. Tompkins designed the Eleven Levels house in 1907. Atterbury was a prominent Yale-educated architect who specialized in "weekend homes of the wealthy." Several pictures of Eleven Levels were featured in a 1919 issue of the *Architectural Review*.

In 1941, Joseph M. Shapiro bought the place. Few people recognize his name, but almost everyone has heard of what he created: the Simplicity Pattern Company.

When Shapiro came to the United States in 1912, his first jobs were as a laborer and a mechanic, though he had been trained in chemistry in his native Russia. Eventually, he became an advertising salesman for a women's magazine that had included designs for making dresses and other articles of clothing at home. In 1927, he decided that dress patterns were too expensive and too complicated, so he started producing his own more simple designs and selling them at first for ten cents instead of the forty-five cents to two dollars that was common at the time for magazines offering patterns. He once told an interviewer that he had asked himself, "What is the tendency of the American people in everything: in architecture, in eating, in living?" The answer, he said, was "simplicity."

"I was pretty sure cheap patterns would go," he continued. "But I made one mistake. Ten cents was *too* cheap. No one would believe they could be any good at that price. So I raised it to 15 cents, and they began selling like hot cakes."

By the time of Shapiro's death in 1968, the Simplicity Pattern Company had an annual volume of $25 to $30 million, selling more than 120 million patterns a year. The company had some four thousand employees and even owned a paper mill to produce the paper on which it printed the patterns. He headed Simplicity from 1927 until 1949 and was chairman of the board until 1967. On his desk, he kept a sign that said, "Fools invent fashions—Wise men follow them."

His wife, Nora Shapiro, established the Ridgefield Toy Clinic, which refurbished donated toys that were then given to needy families; it was based at the Community Center for many years.

The Shapiros contributed much money to museums, educational institutions and charities. They sold the place in 1952 to Paul and Elizabeth Arnold, who had founded the large bakery bearing their name to this day. The Arnolds began their business in 1940, baking two-dozen loaves of bread in a brick oven at their home in Stamford.

The Arnolds sold the estate to Jerry Tuccio in 1959. A year later, Tuccio, who lived for many years in the main Eleven Levels house, applied to the town Planning Commission for the sixty-two lots on one hundred acres. A protracted battle ensued between the officials and the developer over the number and size of the lots. During the debate, Tuccio maintained he was being unfairly denied his right to develop his land reasonably and, at one point, uttered the exclamation, much quoted at the time, "This is Ridgefield and not Russia!"

Shapiro, who'd fled Russia, would certainly have agreed.

RESTING AT THE TWIN MAPLES

Even little pieces of leftover roadway can wind up with names of their own. Along Route 33, Wilton Road West, there is a roadside area that often seems piled with brush and various highway debris. It doesn't look like much, but that sliver of land south of Woodchuck Lane has a history—and a name—attached to it.

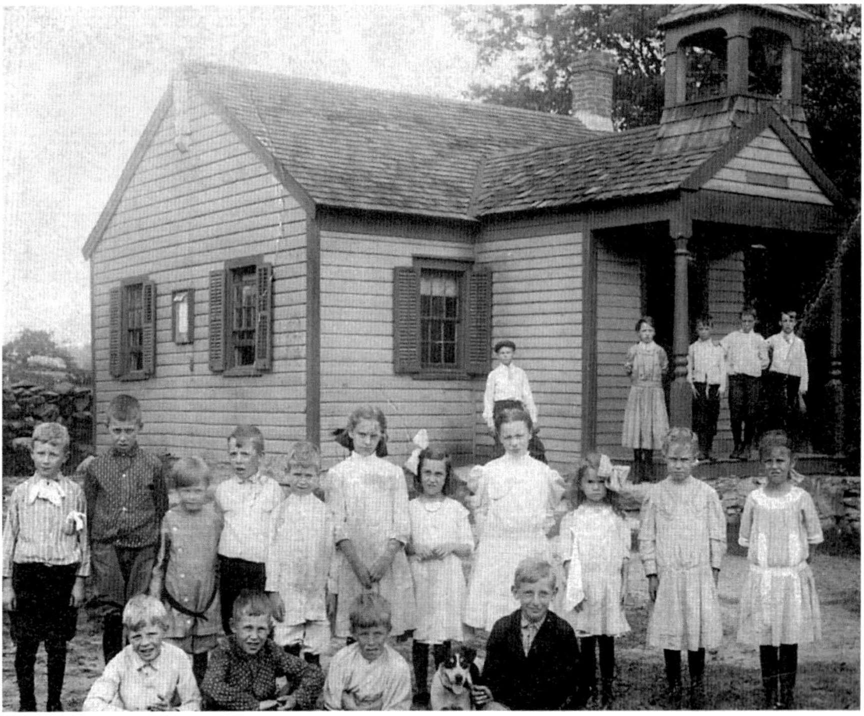

The Flat Rock Schoolhouse and its young scholars are shown here around 1910. The building stood on Wilton Road West, where the state has a pull-off that was once called Twin Maples. *Courtesy of Dorothy Gay Enquist.*

Back in the nineteenth century, part of this little property was the "front yard" of the Flat Rock Schoolhouse, built around 1845. The Flat Rock School District served kids who lived along Wilton Road West, St. John's Road, southern Silver Spring Road and southern Wilton Road East. The schoolhouse closed in 1915, when Flat Rock was consolidated with other districts, and the pupils attended classes in what is today the "old high school" on East Ridge; they were "bused" there in a horse-drawn wagon. The schoolhouse was razed in 1928.

In the 1920s or early '30s, the State Highway Department, which had taken control of Wilton Road West, did some straightening of the highway, leaving behind that sliver of unused land and roadway, which the state put to a new use. The automobile was becoming increasing popular, and many motorists were exploring the more accessible rural countryside. To encourage tourism, Connecticut established many pocket rest areas alongside state roads. Each had a paved pull-off, a grassy area with some picnic tables, a trashcan or two and often some grills for cooking. Motorists could plan a day in the country, bringing along a picnic lunch to enjoy at any of scores of these tiny roadside "parks." Each had its own name, and the one here was called "Twin Maples."

Around 1980, the state gave up on Twin Maples as a rest area; people depositing household trash in the cans had become the chief users. State crews removed the tables, grills, sign and, of course, misused cans.

Other roadside rest areas once existed along Route 7. One, opposite what is now the Days Inn, is right on the Ridgefield-Redding line within Redding and still exists, used mostly by long-haul truckers for spending the night. Amenities like the picnic tables were removed long ago; the expense of maintaining them was not worth the little use to which they were put.

Another rest area existed along the west side of Route 7 north of the Wooster Mountain Gun Club in Danbury. The widening of the highway there to four lanes removed the last traces of it.

2

Names Worth Knowing

The Woman Who Built a Landmark

Ridgefield had many notable "summer residents"—New Yorkers who built weekend and vacation retreats that, more often than not, qualified as mansions. Emily Eaton Hepburn was among the more remarkable of these part-time Ridgefielders, but her accomplishments have been largely overlooked locally. A prominent figure in New York City's intellectual, civic and business scene over a half century, Emily Hepburn, at the age of sixty-one, built one of New York's landmark hotels. The *New York Times* once called her "a real estate novice who created one of New York's most distinctive skyscrapers."

The Vermont native was an 1886 graduate of Saint Lawrence University in Canton, New York, where she met her husband, Alonzo Barton Hepburn, then a lawyer and state banking official. He became a leading New York City banker and was named United States comptroller of the currency by President Benjamin Harrison.

The *Ridgefield Press* took note of their impending arrival in May 1908. "Mr. A.B. Hepburn, one of the most prominent financiers of the country, former comptroller of the currency and now president of the Chase National Bank of New York, is building one of the most handsome homes to be seen in this town of beautiful homes," the newspaper said.

The report was a bit misleading. Emily, not Barton, was actually overseeing the design and construction of Altnacraig, a magnificent mansion on High Ridge whose name could be translated as "high rock." The building later

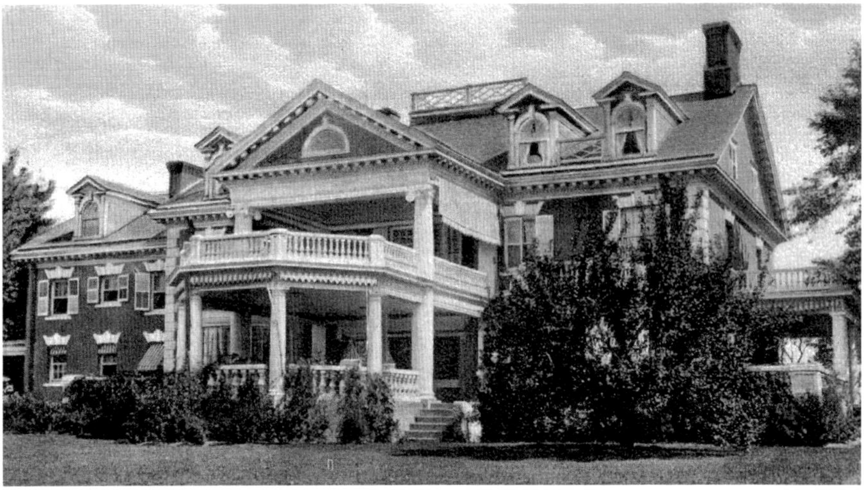

The rear of Altnacraig looked out over forty miles of the Hudson Valley and beyond. *Postcard in author's collection.*

became a well-known nursing home, also called Altnacraig, whose residents included suffragist Alice Paul (see page 65). Altnacraig burned to the ground in a suspicious 1994 blaze and was replaced with a house of similar size.

The Hepburns had many friends in the arts, including Frederic Remington, whom Barton is said to have brought to Ridgefield (see page 53–54). Novelist and journalist Irving Bachellor introduced the Hepburns to Mark Twain, who lived at Stormfield, his estate in nearby Redding. The 1952 biography of Emily Hepburn, "Daughter of Vermont," reports that when the Hepburns arrived at Stormfield for the first time, they were greeted by the yapping of Twain's dog, and before even introductions took place, the author told them, "This is my dog; whatever he does is law in this house." Soon after, the dog got hold of Barton's brand-new hat and took off with it, prompting Twain to point to the motto over his mantelpiece, "Life is just one damned thing after another."

Like his hat, Barton met an unlucky end. He was run over by a bus while crossing a city street in 1922. Worth millions in today's money, "he was benefactor to Hepburn Hospital in Ogdensburg, N.Y., and six libraries in St. Lawrence County, N.Y., all of which are named for him," reports St. Lawrence University, where his and Emily's family papers now reside and where, today, Hepburn Hall recalls the couple who donated the academic building used for economics and government classes.

Emily Hepburn had long been active in civic and charitable organizations, including the New York Botanical Garden, City History Club for children,

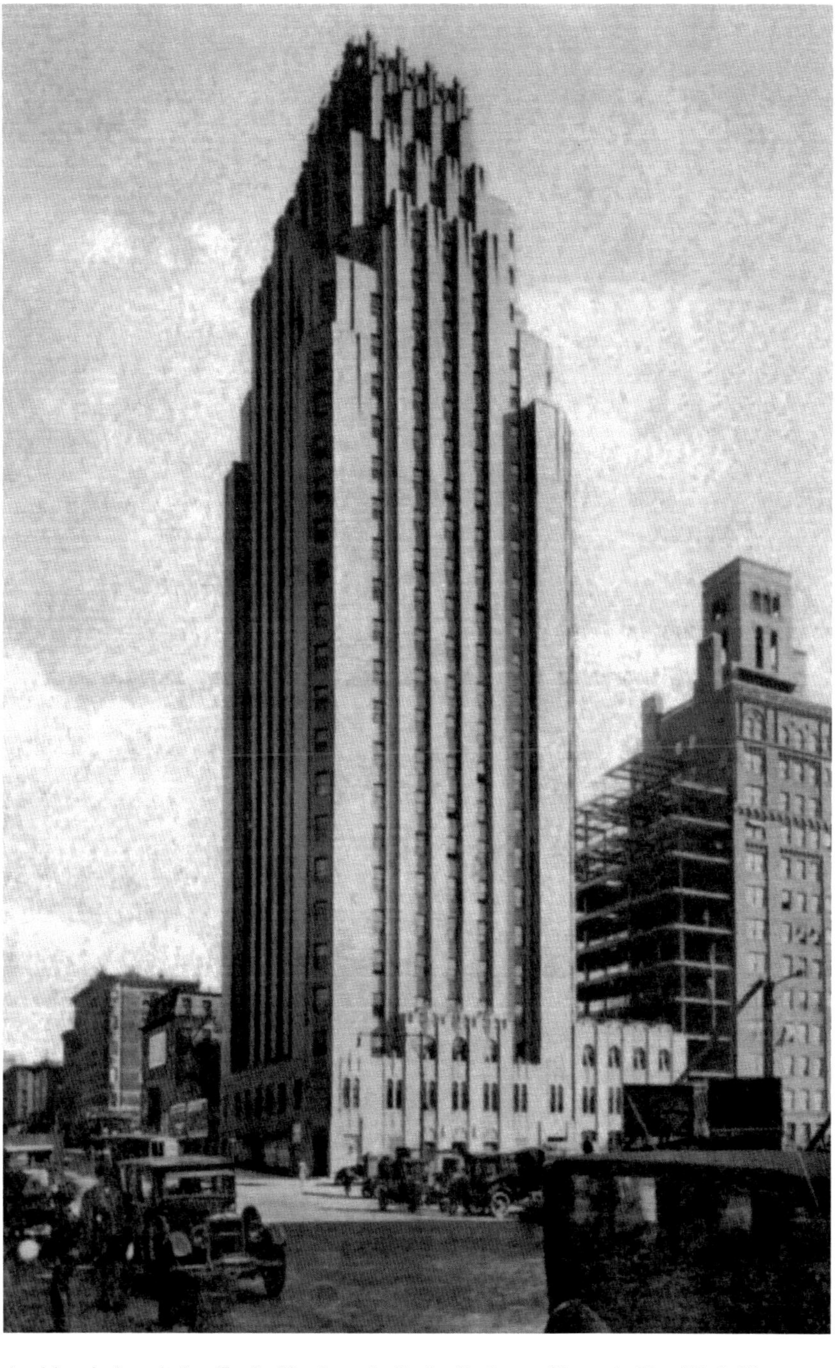

A widow in her sixties, Emily Hepburn built the Beekman Tower in New York City as a residential hotel for young career women. *Old postcard image.*

Inwood House girls reformatory and the New York Infirmary for Women and Children. Here, she was a member of the Ridgefield Garden Club, a group that both beautified and promoted the town. She was also active in the suffrage movement, and after women had won the right to vote, she addressed a new need in New York: housing for young, working women. After the war, many recent college-graduate women were coming to New York to seek careers. In 1924, Hepburn and several others built the American Woman's Association, a high-rise residence for working women, at 353 West Fifty-seventh Street.

Hepburn was dissatisfied with the result, however, and on her own, planned a better building with a more modern architect. "The boxy, unornamented American Woman's Association clubhouse had been simple to the point of drab, the 'International Style' with a migraine, designed by the otherwise traditionalist Benjamin Wistar Morris," wrote Christopher Gray in the *Times*. "Mrs. Hepburn went to John Mead Howells, son of American author William Dean Howells, and a graduate of the École des Beaux-Arts."

Hepburn almost single-handedly set about gaining support for the project, including selling stock (one of the stock purchasers was Sara Roosevelt, mother of Franklin Delano Roosevelt). The result was the 380-room Panhellenic House at First Avenue and East Forty-ninth Street, completed in 1928 and described in early promotional brochures as "a club-hotel for women." The twenty-eight-story, orange brick building is considered one of the great Art Deco skyscrapers in New York.

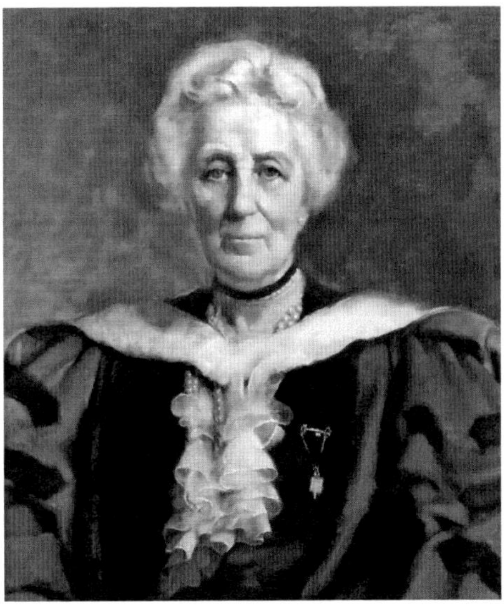

A portrait of Emily Eaton Hepburn in her St. Lawrence University academic garb was painted by Cleonebel Jacobs. *Courtesy of St. Lawrence University.*

"I wanted to prove that women could do big business," Hepburn once said about her late-blooming career. The quotation appears in *Daughter of Vermont* four years before her death.

The hotel was not just a residence but also a place where women could, in today's parlance, "network" and learn from one another. One supporter of the project called it "a training school for leadership, a mental exchange" for women.

Hepburn, who also built and lived in an apartment building at nearby 2 Beekman Place, found occupancy rates declining during the Depression and opened the building to men as well as women, renaming it the Beekman Tower Hotel. The hotel continued in business until 2013, when it was converted to long-term residential suites.

The Beekman, incidentally, is a block from the United Nations. The *Times* once reported that, "according to legend," Hepburn "persuaded the Rockefellers to buy the East River land for the United Nations." How's that for good business sense?

MR. HERRICK'S "HELICOPTER"

Three doors north of the Hepburns' Altnacraig on High Ridge was the less stately but still sizable home of Gerardus Post Herrick. Long before the military developed vertical takeoff and landing aircraft, like the Osprey, this lawyer-engineer had invented an aircraft that did just that.

Gerardus Herrick, who generally went by the name of Gerard, was a rather eccentric but talented lawyer and a skilled research engineer. Born in 1873, he was a member of the thirteenth generation of the Post family to live in New York City since the clan arrived in 1654. He graduated from Princeton and became a lawyer. After serving as a captain in World War I in the army air service—not as a pilot but as a gunnery officer—he came up with the idea of a convertible aircraft that could fly either fixed-wing like a conventional plane or vertically as an "autogyro." In the 1920s and 1930s, he partnered with a couple of aircraft manufacturers to build a working model of his autogyro.

"The first aircraft, the HV-1, was ready on Nov. 6, 1931," the Smithsonian Institution says. "The test pilot, Merrill Lambert, made several successful test flights in both fixed- and rotating-wing mode, but when he attempted an in-flight transition between the two, the aircraft fell out of control and crashed. Lambert bailed out of the aircraft, but was killed when his parachute failed to open." However, an analysis of the accident found the basic design was sound, and Herrick continued to develop what he called a "vertiplane."

The plane was a fixed-wing monoplane with a large overhead propeller, shaped somewhat like a smaller wing. The aircraft could take off as a monoplane and once in the air, convert to a hovering aircraft using the large

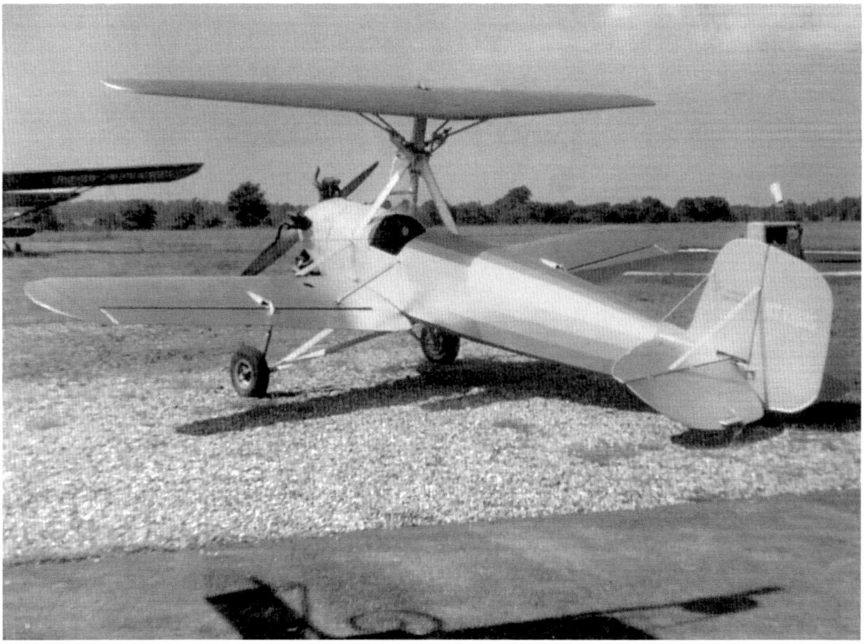

The top "wing" on Herrick's HV-2a was a rotor that lifted the plane nearly straight up. *Smithsonian National Air and Space Museum (NASM 9A06274).*

overhead propeller. It could then land in a very small area. The aircraft could also take off vertically, but it could not convert to horizontal flight in mid-air and had to remain a "helicopter" until it landed.

A new version, the HV-2a, began flying successfully in 1936, cruising at one hundred miles per hour as a fixed-wing plane and sixty-five miles per hour in autogyro mode. The 2,300-pound aircraft needed only sixty feet of runway to take off. Unfortunately, the aircraft's "remarkable performance did not justify production as the weight penalties imposed by carrying both rotary and fixed wing structures eliminated its commercial advantage over conventional airplanes," the Smithsonian said.

Herrick continued to work on convertible airplane ideas and unsuccessfully tried to gain investor and government support until his death in 1955. He didn't limit his interests to aircraft, however, and over the years, the attorney/engineer wrote a manual for small-arms instructors and did research work into blast furnaces, steam engines, lenses and rifle sights.

"Gerard Post Herrick was one of the earliest to advocate combining fixed-wing flight with rotary-wing flight," wrote Dr. Bruch H. Charnov in a study of the inventor. "He has been given little notice by vertical flight historians, quite unjustifiably becoming one of the forgotten rotary-wing pioneers, the champion of a concept that even today in various forms seeks legitimacy."

He and his wife, Lois, had their home in Ridgefield starting in the 1920s. A large garage in the back once housed the HV-2a, Dick Venus recalled. After Lois Herrick died in 1983, Venus was at an estate sale on the property when he came across "the largest propeller that I had ever seen, lying on the floor of the garage. No doubt this enormous thing could lift a house right off the ground if you had a machine with the energy to turn it." He concluded it was a spare propeller for the HV-2a, which had already been donated to the Smithsonian Institution.

Incidentally, Herrick was a cousin of Myron T. Herrick, the U.S. ambassador to France who greeted Charles Lindbergh on his arrival in Paris in 1927. Myron must have been popular: he's the only American ambassador to France with a street in Paris named after him—Avenue Myron Herrick.

BEHIND THE SCENES OF THE SAIGON RESCUE

It was helicopters that helped Paul C. Velte Jr. lead a historic rescue operation.

Velte had led a quiet life in Ridgefield, serving as a scoutmaster, a church building committee chairman and even a justice of the peace. But his last job was anything but quiet. Working for the CIA, he orchestrated the evacuation of more than one thousand Americans in the final hours of the U.S. presence in Vietnam.

Velte was CEO of Air America, a large airline that was secretly owned by the Central Intelligence Agency and used for a variety of missions in Southeast Asia. During the war years, Air America had flown civilians, diplomats, spies, doctors, refugees, commandos, drug enforcement agents, injured soldiers and even the likes of Richard M. Nixon. But its last mission was rescuing Americans from Saigon as the city was about to fall to North Vietnamese troops.

On April 29, 1975, the South Vietnamese capital became the scene of what has been called the largest helicopter evacuation in history. "Two United States Marine Corps helicopter squadrons, ten U.S. Air Force helicopters, and Air America carried out 1,373 Americans and 5,595 people of other nationalities," wrote William Leary and E. Merton Coulter in *MHQ*, a military history magazine.

Velte didn't direct operations from the headquarters in Washington. He was on the ground in Vietnam, often in situations where he, his pilots and staff were under fire, such as at Tan Son Nhut airport just outside the city. He planned to supply twenty-eight Air America Bell UH-1 "Huey" helicopters that were light enough to land on buildings; the larger marine copters, used for most of the evacuation flights, were too heavy for many buildings to support.

"Because of a shortage of pilots, many of these helicopters would have to be flown by a single pilot," Leary and Coulter wrote. "According to the U.S. Air Force account of the final evacuation, 'This was risky, but Air America was accustomed to such risks and expressed no reservations about that aspect of the Saigon air evacuation.'"

Velte had to deal with not only enemy fire but also political and other problems. U.S. ambassador Graham Martin hesitated for days to act on evacuation planning. There was a lack of adequate fuel to keep the Hueys going. The military refused to protect Air America's helicopters, and the North Vietnamese subsequently stole some of those undefended aircraft. In mid-April, Velte had tried to get the air force to arrange for an aircraft carrier to be offshore to serve as an operating base in case his helicopters were needed for the evacuation and the Tan Son Nhut was under attack or overtaken.

"The baby carrier," he told the air force, "had the necessary machine shops to do repair work, had fuel, and had mobility. It could move up and down the coast and would allow Air America to perform its missions as required."

An air force general said the carrier could not be provided but then tried to arrange for thirty marine pilots to serve as copilots on the Air America helicopters. Ambassador Martin, reluctant to admit Saigon was about to fall, vetoed the plan for copilots. Martin was later criticized for delaying the evacuation planning and execution—even though most of South Vietnam had already fallen to the north. "Faced with imminent disaster," Secretary of State Henry Kissinger wrote, "Martin decided to go down with the ship…I considered Martin's stonewalling dangerous."

In the end, Air America, down to around thirteen helicopters, still managed to evacuate more than one thousand Americans to offshore ships or to locations on land where the bigger marine copters could ferry them to vessels. "That was no small accomplishment, to be sure," said a CIA analyst named Frank Snepp, "particularly in view of the fact that the maximum capacity of each Huey was barely 12 people."

According to David Wilson, a Velte grandson, his grandfather "was on the last helicopter out of Saigon with nothing but a .45 pistol and a pair of underwear."

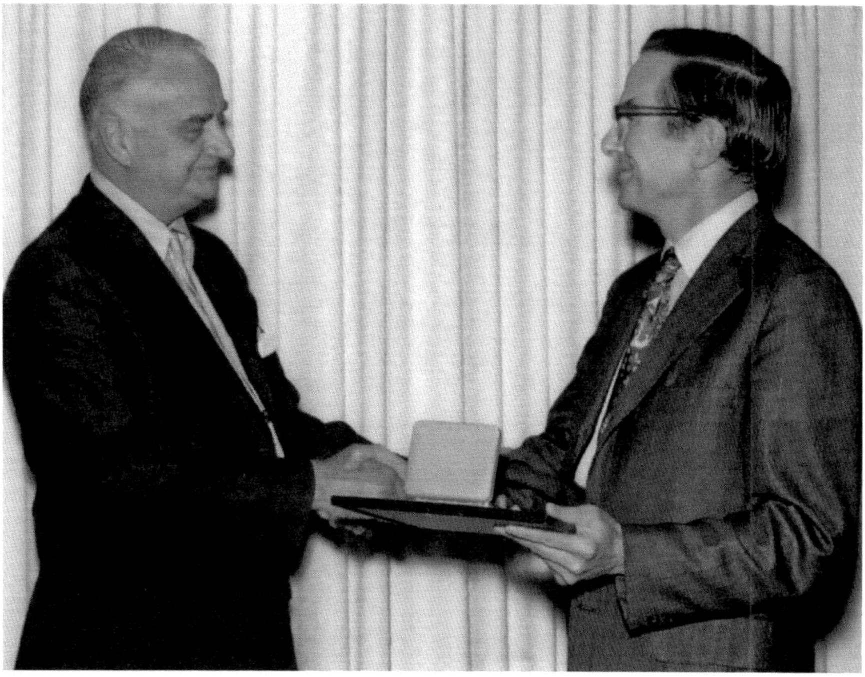

Paul C. Velte Jr. (left) is shown receiving a commendation from a Central Intelligence Agency official for his service with Air America in Southeast Asia. *Courtesy of Paul J. Velte IV.*

The end of the Vietnam conflict also spelled the end of Air America. On May 5, 1975, CIA director William Colby cabled Velte: "The withdrawal from Vietnam draws to a conclusion Air America's operational activities." He added a few words of praise for the staff. "Air America, appropriately named, has served its country well," he said.

However, "the pilots never heard even that modest accolade," wrote Leary and Coulter. "The CIA would not publicly acknowledge its ownership of the airline for another year, and it would not issue a commendation to these secret soldiers of the Cold War until 2001."

A native of New York City, Paul Christian Velte Jr. was a Pace College graduate and World War II navy veteran who had worked as an executive for Pan American Airlines before joining Air America. He was based in Taipei, Taiwan, and later at the main Air America headquarters in Washington, but he also maintained a home in Ridgefield from 1955 until his death at age sixty-two in 1976—the same year the CIA officially dissolved Air America.

His contributions to aviation were recognized in *Who's Who in America*, but his contribution to the largest helicopter evacuation in history has gone largely unnoticed or unheralded. He is buried in Ridgebury Cemetery, where a small monument marks his grave.

THE LAST DAYS OF FREDERIC REMINGTON

Another Ridgefielder who experienced wild times had a far different profession and gained far more fame. Frederic Remington's pictures and sculptures depicting the Old West are in countless museums and collections

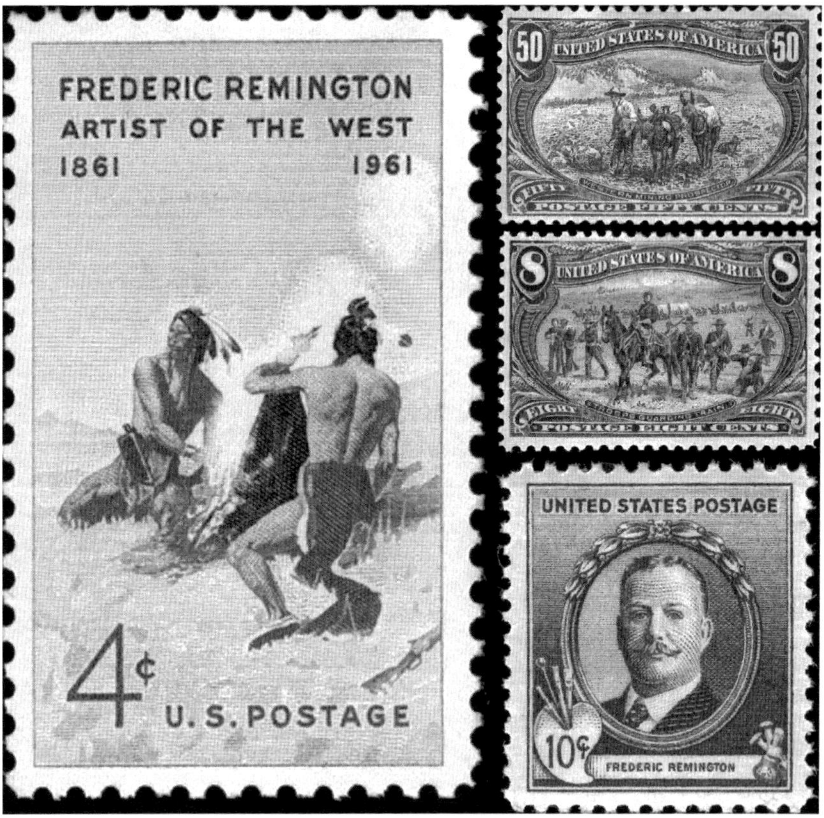

Four of the six Remington stamps. *Left*: honoring his 100th birthday with a scene from *Smoke Signal*; *upper right*: two 1898 stamps that made use of his illustrations; *lower right*: his portrait on a 1940 issue in the "Famous Americans" series. *United States Postal Service.*

and bring large prices. A Remington sculpture, a bronze called *The Wounded Bunkie*, sold at auction for $5.6 million in 2008 while an oil painting, *A Reconnaissance*, fetched $5.2 million at a 1999 auction. Even postal people love him. Few Americans outside presidents like George Washington have been so extensively remembered on United States postage stamps—at least six bear his art or his face.

Unfortunately for Remington, his stay in Ridgefield was brief. He died six months after arriving.

Though his fame is based on the Old West that he so colorfully documented, Frederic Sackrider Remington spent all but a few years of his life in the Northeast. He was born in 1861 in Canton, New York, the son of a newspaper editor who wanted him to pursue that career. While he attended military schools in Vermont and Massachusetts, Remington found he loved to draw more than write or fight and wound up attending the School of Fine Arts at Yale, where he also played football for the Bulldogs. His first published illustration was a cartoon of a "bandaged football player" for a student newspaper. He left Yale when his father became seriously ill and died. With an inheritance in hand, Remington decided against returning to college and headed west in 1881 to seek adventure; he was only nineteen years old. In the next few years, he traveled widely in the western states and territories, working as a cowboy, a sheep rancher, a saloon owner, a reporter and at other jobs—all the while sketching what he was seeing.

Around 1885, he came back east and studied at the Art Students League. His father encouraged him to get a job at the Chase National Bank in New York City, headed by A. Barton Hepburn, whom Remington had known as a boy in Upstate New York. According to a biography of Barton's wife, Emily Eaton Hepburn, "Remington…was more dismayed than pleased. He reported for work as directed, hung up his hat and coat, sat down at his desk and twiddled his pencil over a drawing pad until noon. Then he put on his hat and coat, and left for lunch. He never came back."

Instead, he took some of his drawings of the West to *Harper's Magazine*, where they were immediately purchased for fifty dollars each, and he was hired as an illustrator.

The reason he left the bank job, he later explained to Hepburn, was that he "couldn't add."

He returned to the West briefly to cover the Indian Wars in Apache country for *Harper's*. By then, he was earning $1,200 a year as a commercial artist, a sizable sum then. "That's a pretty good break for an ex cow-puncher," he said.

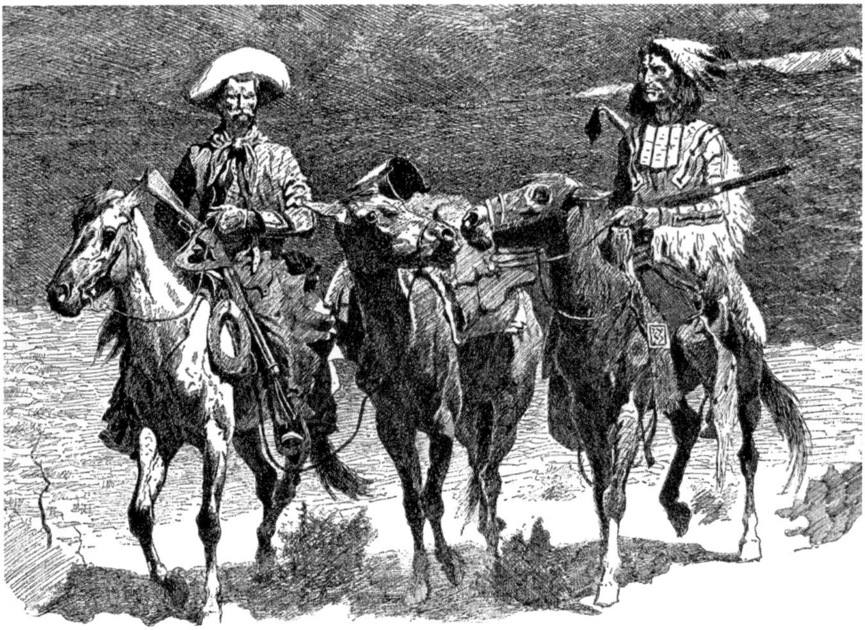

Remington loved to ride and wanted his epitaph to be "He knew the horse." Here's an example of his drawing of the horse, called *A Questionable Companionship*. *From* Harper's Weekly, *August 9, 1890.*

Remington went on to illustrate not only for magazines but also books, and he wound up writing a half dozen books of his own about the West. Virtually all of his illustrations, his paintings and later his sculptures dealt with western themes. "I knew the wild riders and vacant lands were about to vanish forever," he wrote. "And the more I considered the subject, the bigger the forever loomed."

While he became widely praised as an illustrator, Remington wanted recognition as an artist. By the turn of the twentieth century, he was devoting much of his time to painting and sculpture—and even burned many earlier works he felt were too much like illustrations.

Remington was living and working in New Rochelle, New York, when he decided he wanted a wilder environment. (Another noted New Rochelle artist-illustrator later did the same; Norman Rockwell moved first to Vermont and later Stockbridge, Massachusetts.) There are several stories about why Remington chose Ridgefield. One was that the town was recommended by his friend Barton Hepburn; Hepburn had recently built a mansion on High Ridge, called Altnacraig (see page 44). Another explanation was that Poultney Bigelow, a close friend who was editor and founder of *Outing* magazine, had recommended Ridgefield for both its wildness and its sophistication. Bigelow lived in nearby New York State and probably knew the town from visits. Perhaps both Hepburn and Bigelow had talked up the town to Remington, who at the same time was being strongly influenced by the Impressionist movement—and a leading impressionist, J. Alden Weir, lived in Ridgefield and was often visited by Remington's impressionist friend Childe Hassam.

Remington wound up buying forty-two acres along Barry Avenue, on which he and his wife, Eva, designed a sizable home and a state-of-the-art studio that featured a huge fieldstone fireplace and large (for the era) plate glass windows. The estate was known as Lural Place, according to his *Ridgefield Press* obituary, but another source said he called it "One Hoss Farm." After his death, the estate became known as Oak Knoll, a name that has stuck over the decades since.

Remington moved into the home in July 1909. In December, he fell ill and was eventually diagnosed with appendicitis that developed into peritonitis. His condition was said to have been exacerbated by his treating himself with laxatives and the fact that he weighed three hundred pounds. An emergency operation was performed at his house—reportedly on the dining room table. As the *Press* reported at the time, "The artist rallied after the operation and it was believed he would recover. Complications, however, entered into the case on Saturday and the patient sank rapidly during the night." He died on Sunday, the day after Christmas. He was only forty-eight years old.

During his career, Remington produced more than three thousand drawings, illustrations, paintings and bronzes. "The extent of what he might have been was curtailed only by his untimely death at a time when he could have had 20 years of growth ahead of him, but he was already the paramount exponent of his kind of art and the most American of them all," said biographers Peggy and Harold Samuels.

Remington loved riding and depicting horses in action, be it on canvass or in bronze. "When I die," he told a friend not long before his death, "I want my epitaph to be, 'He knew the horse.'" However, his spare gravestone in Canton, New York, bears only his name and the years of his birth and death.

In 1965, Remington's house was declared a National Historic Landmark. The studio he had in the house has been reproduced in detail at the Remington Art Museum in Ogdensburg, New York, where his family once lived. Although Remington lived here and died here, not one of his paintings or sculptures is known to exist in Ridgefield.

For years, townspeople had wanted a road name recalling the artist. From shortly after his death until well into the 1950s, various movements tried to have Barry Avenue changed to Remington Road. In fact, a 1927 map of property along Barry Avenue called the highway "Remington Road."

A new road at the 1960s Westmoreland subdivision gave the town a perfect opportunity to commemorate the artist: Remington Road runs between Barry Avenue and Peaceable Hill Road, intersecting Barry Avenue not far from Remington's house. Perhaps the artist had once hunted on the Westmoreland estate.

THE MAN BEHIND ST. STEPHEN'S—AND COLUMBIA

The scholarly missionary who established the Episcopal church in Ridgefield was also the man behind the founding of one of this country's oldest and most prestigious universities.

For nearly a century, Connecticut had only one official practicing religion: Congregational. However, in the early 1700s, the tiny Church of England in Connecticut, with help from the mother country, established a congregation in Stratford. Reverend Samuel Johnson, pastor at Stratford, then began acting as a missionary to a dozen or more Connecticut towns.

In Ridgefield, Dr. Johnson established a congregation in 1725 that grew into St. Stephen's Episcopal Church. According to old church records, he "preached there occasionally for several years, and was instrumental in bringing several families into the church."

Soon, others took over in Ridgefield, and Johnson eventually became the top Episcopal minister in the state (until 1728, he had been Connecticut's *only* Episcopal minister).

The Guilford native graduated from Yale in 1714 and started out a Congregational minister, converting in 1723; he sailed to London for his ordination at St. Martin-in-the-Fields Church. He was a "high church" Episcopalian who, as St. Stephen's historian Robert Haight put it, "stressed the Catholic side of the church's tradition."

As early as 1750, Dr. Johnson was corresponding with Benjamin Franklin about establishing a new kind of college in New York. He began working with his wife's family, former students and Trinity Church in New York City to found a school. A board of trustees was formed and, in 1752, nominated him to be the college's first president. The board decided to call the school King's College—to help gain a royal charter from King George II.

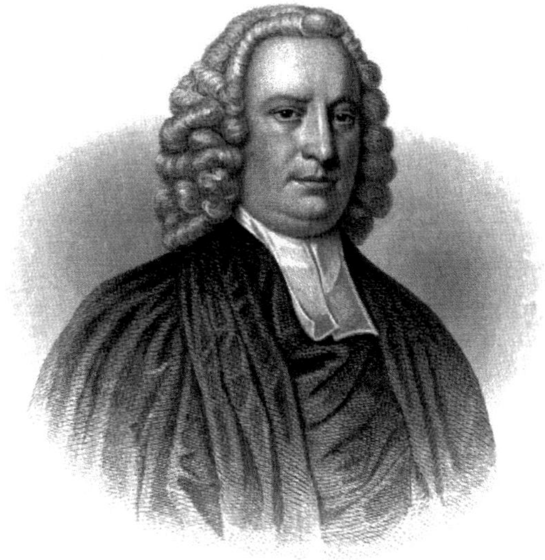

Dr. Samuel Johnson helped establish St. Stephen's Church and later led the founding of Columbia University. *Engraving in* Life and Correspondence of Samuel Johnson, D.D. *by E.E. Beardsley, 1874, based on a painting by John Smybert.*

Between 1750 and 1753, Dr. Johnson and Dr. Franklin designed a "new-model" plan for an American college that would be used at King's. It was profession-oriented, classes were taught in English instead of Latin, professors specialized in one subject and there would be no religious test for admission. The curriculum included math, science, history, commerce, government and nature.

The charter was obtained in 1754. Johnson himself taught the first class of eight students; he included use of his own textbook on philosophy. Thirty years later, in the wake of the Revolution, the school dropped the "King" and selected Columbia as its name. The university is the oldest in New York State and fifth oldest in the United States.

Over his career, Dr. Johnson wrote nearly three dozen books. He has been called by various historians "a towering intellect of colonial America, a man of great curiosity and philosophical interests," "the most erudite colonial Anglican theologian of the eighteenth century" and the "first important philosopher in colonial America." He died in 1772.

Incidentally, a son, William Samuel Johnson, was a signer of the U.S. Constitution; he chaired the Constitution's five-member Committee of Style, which framed the final text of the document. He also became the third president of Columbia.

FANNY'S SONGS AND HUBERT'S TUNES

While Dr. Johnson was a leader in the intellectual side of religion, three Ridgefielders were in the forefront of a more emotional side: sacred music.

Among the most famous hymn writers of all time was Fanny Crosby, a blind woman who spent her formative years in Ridgefield. She wrote thousands of hymns, including "Blessed Assurance," "Safe in the Arms of Jesus," "Praise Him! Praise Him!" and "Close to Thee."

Born in 1820 in Brewster, New York, Jane "Fanny" Crosby was blinded at six weeks by a disease. A few months later, her father died, leaving her twenty-one-year-old mother a widow. Fanny and her mother came to Ridgefield when Fanny was nine, living with Mr. and Mrs. Elijah Hawley on Main Street on the south corner of Branchville Road in a house that's no longer there.

"Mrs. Hawley, a kind Christian lady…who had no children of her own, became deeply interested in me, and under her supervision I acquired a thorough knowledge of the Bible," Crosby wrote in one of her two autobiographies. "She gave me a number of chapters each week to learn, sometimes as many as five…and at the end of the first 12 months, I could repeat a large portion of the first four books of the Old Testament and the four Gospels." In fact, she was so good at memorizing that she was presented with a Bible that year in Sunday school for reciting more verses than any other pupil.

"The good Mrs. Hawley was kind in every respect and sought to teach me many practical lessons that I now remember with gratitude and affection," Crosby wrote, adding that one of those lessons was the tale of George Washington and the cherry tree.

When Crosby was about fifteen, she left Ridgefield to attend the New York Institute for the Blind. Soon after graduation from the institute in 1843, Crosby worked as a lobbyist in Washington, D.C., pleading for support of education for the blind. There she became the first woman to speak in the U.S. Senate. She then appeared before the joint houses of Congress, offering this poem:

O ye, who here from every state convene,
Illustrious band! may we not hope the scene
You now behold will prove to every mind
Instruction hath a ray to cheer the blind.

She soon joined the teaching staff of the New York Institute for the Blind.

Her writing career started with nonreligious poetry; she produced four books of secular poems. While teaching at the institute, she became friends with Grover Cleveland, then a fellow teacher, though only seventeen

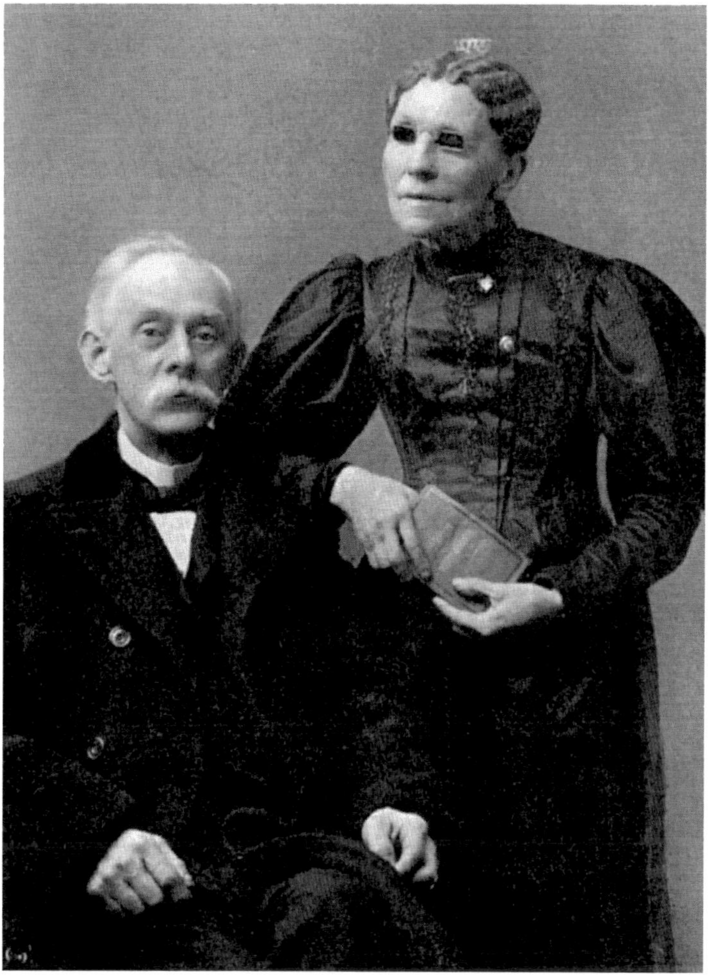

Hubert Platt Main and Fanny Crosby were close friends and music partners. Both lived in Ridgefield as children. *From* Fanny Crosby's Story of Ninety-Four Years *by S. Trevenna Jackson (1915).*

years old. The two spent much time together after classes, and the future U.S. president often wrote down poems that Crosby dictated to him.

Her poetry writing soon led to song writing, though most were at first secular—or, as she called them, "people's songs." She wrote political songs, patriotic songs (especially during the Civil War) and even cantatas. During the war, she began writing religious songs, both under her own name and under pseudonyms, and over her career, she penned the lyrics to more than eight thousand hymns. Crosby once said she wanted her hymns to win one

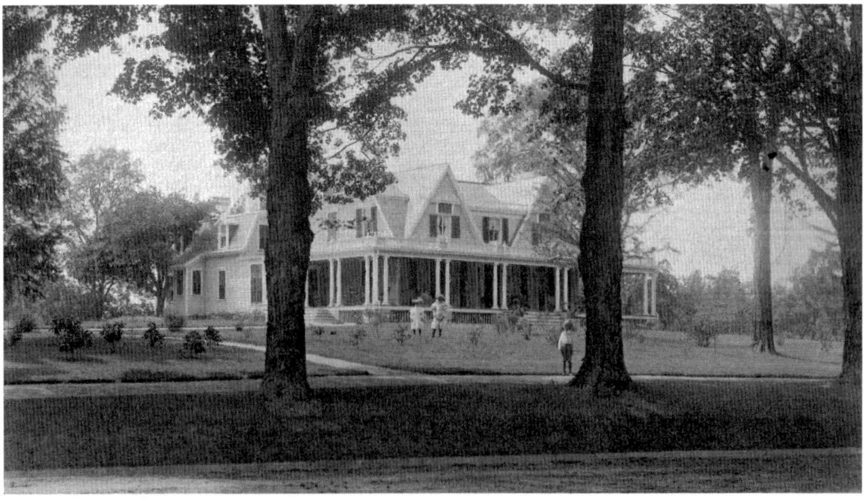

Graeloe, the house of music publisher Lucius H. Biglow, stood in what's now Ballard Park. Biglow's daughter, Elizabeth Ballard, ordered the house razed when she bequeathed the property to the town as a park. *Circa 1910 postcard in author's collection.*

million souls for Christ, and her words were certainly available to many more than that. Books containing her lyrics are said to have sold at least 100 million copies.

Biglow and Main of New York City, one of the first publishers of sacred music, distributed many of Crosby's hymns. Biglow was Lucius Horatio Biglow, who, in 1889, bought an eighteenth-century house on Main Street in Ridgefield to create a fine retreat from the city. When Elizabeth Biglow Ballard, his daughter, died in 1964, she bequeathed that estate to the town. Today, it is Ballard Park.

The "Main" of Biglow and Main was Sylvester Main, born in Ridgefield in 1817 and a childhood friend of Fanny Crosby. "Among the playmates who used to gather on the village green was Sylvester Main who was two or three years older than I," Crosby recalled. "He was a prime favorite with the gentler sex, for he used to protect us from the annoyances of more mischievous boys."

Sylvester Main became a singing school teacher and wound up in New York City, compiling books of hymn music. He went to work for William Bradbury, music publisher and hymnist, and when Bradbury died around 1868, he and Lucius Biglow partnered to take over the firm, calling it Biglow and Main.

The Ridgefield connections don't end there. Sylvester's son, Hubert Platt Main, was also born in Ridgefield and, as a young man, compiled books of music, was a choir leader and organist in churches and eventually joined Biglow and Main. He composed more than one thousand works, including the music for hundreds of popular hymns of the mid-nineteenth century, among them "We Shall Meet Beyond the River," "Blessed Homeland" and "The Bright Forever"—the words of the last two were written by Fanny Crosby. In the 1915 book *Fanny Crosby's Story of Ninety-Four Years*, she called him "one of my most precious friends." The book includes a picture of the two, seated together, called "Fast Friends" (see page 59).

Fanny Crosby died in 1915 at the age of ninety-four and is buried in Bridgeport. She had been married for a while, but she and her husband eventually separated. The couple had one child, who died as a baby. Hubert Main, who died in 1925, is buried in New Jersey beneath a stone that says, "We shall meet beyond the river."

Two Major Maestros

Ridgefield has been home to noted conductors, too.

Back in the 1960s and '70s, townspeople frequently encountered an elegant, elderly couple strolling the village sidewalks. Many thought they made a cute pair. Few recognized the man as a conductor of most of the world's leading concert and opera orchestras. Over his long career, Frieder Weissmann once estimated, he had contributed to more than four thousand classical music recordings, most of them in Germany in the 1920s.

He was one of two world-class conductors who have lived in Ridgefield.

A native of Germany, Dr. Weissmann was born in 1893; studied at Heidelberg, Munich,

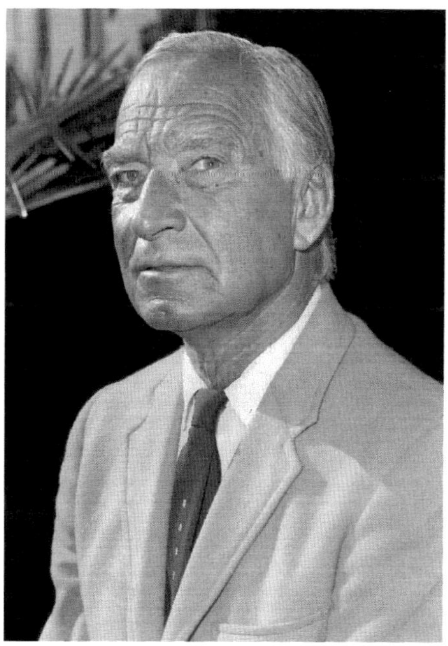

Conductor Frieder Weissmann was known for his thousands of early recordings—and his piercing blue eyes. *From the* Ridgefield Press *archives.*

Grenoble and Geneva; and began his conducting career at the State Opera of Berlin while in his twenties. In 1932 and 1933, he was a guest conductor of the Berlin Philharmonic, which the likes of Brahms, Dvorak, Grieg and Mahler had also led.

But with rising anti-Semitic sentiments in Germany, he left the country in 1933, arriving first in Holland, where he led the Concertgebouw in some concerts, and then spent several years in Argentina, where he met and married his second wife, Rosita "Rose" Chevallier Boutell, an actress and daughter of a well-known Argentine soccer player. (He married his first wife, German opera star Meta Seinemeyer, as she was dying of leukemia at the age of thirty-three.) During the next three decades, he conducted orchestras throughout North and South America, including almost every major American symphony orchestra. In this country, he recorded for such labels as RCA Victor, Decca, Columbia and Odeon. Many of his recordings are still being sold today.

The Weissmanns came to Ridgefield around 1960, summering at the Elms Inn for nine years and then living full-time on Prospect Ridge.

"It is the most secretly guarded, God-given talent which enables you to stand in front of 100 men and without a word, only with the movement of your eyes, evoke from them as from one person the utmost of expression of delight, of harshness, of piano, of forte, of anything that might be contained in human nature," Weissmann said in a 1966 *Ridgefield Press* interview.

Tom Belote, a Ridgefield attorney and historian who knew Weissmann when the conductor lived at the Elms, confirmed the power of the maestro's eyes. "He had blue eyes and used them when he talked to people," Belote recalled. "It was impressive."

Belote added, "He also used his cane in later years as he would have used a conductor's baton. He would wave it while standing on the street to wave down a car for a ride. He would also use it in the restaurant and stamp it in the floor while he was sitting if he wanted something from a waiter."

A frequent traveler and conductor well into his eighties, Weissmann once said, "I'll stop when I am dead."

Rose Weissmann died here in 1980 and is buried in Ridgebury Cemetery. Two years later, Frieder moved to Amsterdam, where he died in 1984 at the age of ninety-one.

Perhaps the better known of Ridgefield's two conductors was Maxim Shostakovich, son of the noted twentieth-century Russian composer Dimitri Shostakovich. While Weissmann left Germany because of the persecution of Jews, Shostakovich left Russia because of the lack of freedom.

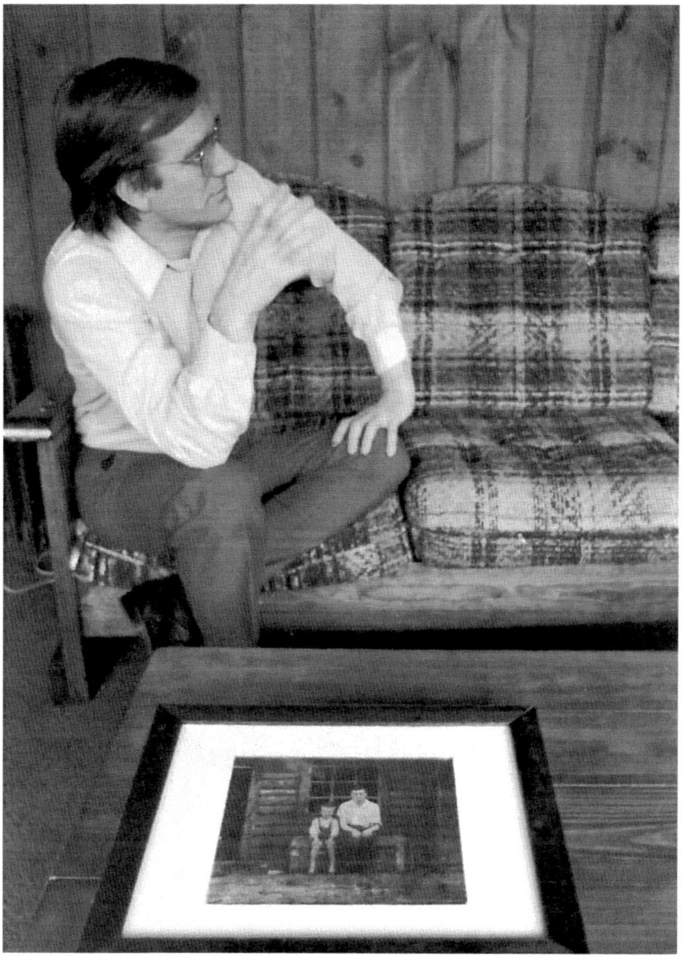

Conductor Maxim Shostakovich, who was interviewed by the *Ridgefield Press* in 1984, fled Russia in 1981 but returned after the fall of communism. In the foreground is a picture of him as a boy with his composer father, Dimitri Shostakovich. *Thomas B. Nash photograph, from the* Ridgefield Press *archives.*

While on a tour in Germany in 1981 with a Russian symphony orchestra, Shostakovich requested and was granted asylum in the United States. He had thought about escaping from Russia, but he hadn't planned to defect at that time. However, when another orchestra member did so, a KGB member traveling with the orchestra told him that the defection meant the whole orchestra would be punished: none of the musicians would be allowed to travel for five years. It was the final straw.

"Just after the last performance was a reception," Shostakovich told reporter Macklin Reid of the *Ridgefield Press* in 1984. "At this reception, also, were members of the German police. I made contact with these policemen in the intermission, during the performance."

The police arranged to have a car waiting outside during the post-concert reception. "It was something like a big terrace, with windows. I opened, with my son, these windows, and went out to the car."

Defection was difficult, he said, "because we have many friends in Russia, and we love our country. But, to be free in the human spirit is much more important."

Soon after he arrived in this country, he moved to Florida Road with his son, Dimitri, who had fled with him.

Born in St. Petersburg (then called Leningrad) in 1938, Maxim Shostakovich soon showed talent as a fine pianist, but he already knew he wanted to be a conductor. "So I asked my father about this," he told an interviewer a few years ago. "He said, 'That's fine. But other things must come first.' He was always kind and helpful. I used to play two-piano music with him, and I got to know a lot of works that way."

Having mastered the piano, he studied conducting at the Moscow Conservatory. In 1957, Maxim played the first performance of his father's Second Piano Concerto, which the father had written expressly for the son. In April 1984, Maxim's son, Dimitri, played that same concerto while Maxim led the Ridgefield Symphony Orchestra on the stage of Ridgefield High School. "I love to conduct my father's music, because it's my duty," he told the *Press* at the time. "It's native music for me, and I'm very happy to conduct it."

Shostakovich has led almost every major orchestra in the United States and Europe and, while in Ridgefield, was conductor and music director of the New Orleans Symphony for five years.

He entertained many Russian expatriates and artist friends from New York at his country home. "I have many friends—artists, sculptors, musicians—who come during the weekend," he said.

Shostakovich moved to Redding in 1991. In 1994, after the dissolution of the Soviet Union and the institution of a democratic Russian government, he flew to his native country to conduct a concert in St. Petersburg. He soon decided to return to his home city of St. Petersburg to live.

In 1984, he had not been optimistic about going home. "It's impossible for us now," he said then. "If things change in our country, it's possible that, someday, we'll see our country again." He was probably surprised at how soon "someday" was.

PAUL STAMPED, THEN COINED

While a half dozen Ridgefield residents have been honored on United States postage stamps, only one has made it onto a U.S. coin. And Alice Paul did so in a rather unusual fashion.

Very few faces appear on circulating U.S. coins, outside of presidents, eagles and depictions of "Liberty." However, the U.S. Mint also issues a few commemorative coins that honor people, places, events and institutions. "Although these coins are legal tender, they are not minted for general circulation," the mint says. "Each commemorative coin is produced by the United States Mint in limited quantity and is only available for a limited time."

In 2007, the mint began producing what it calls "the First Spouse Coins." Each is aimed at honoring the wife of a president of the United States, and each was issued at the same time that their husbands were honored on circulating one-dollar coins, minted in the Presidential Coin Series. A problem was that some presidents had no spouses when they were in office—no "first ladies," as they have been commonly called. One of those spouseless presidents was Chester A. Arthur, whose beloved wife, Ellen, died in 1880, a year before he took office.

Arthur was elected vice president under James A. Garfield and assumed that office in 1881. In July, only a few months later, Garfield was shot. In September, the president died of his wounds, and Arthur became the nation's twenty-first president. He filled out the term and, in declining health, chose not to run for another term.

Mint officials decided to find a woman who would be appropriate as a "first spouse" coin corresponding to Chester Arthur. They picked suffragist Alice Paul, who had a home on Branchville Road in Ridgefield for many years. Dr. Paul—she had doctorates in economics and law—was probably the leading voice for woman's suffrage in the early twentieth century. Once the right to vote was obtained, she spent the rest of her long life fighting for the Equal Rights Amendment to the U.S. Constitution, which she and Crystal Eastman wrote, to guarantee equal rights for women. (While it passed both houses of Congress, it was ratified by only thirty-five of the thirty-eight states. Needless to say, Connecticut, home of many leading suffragists, was among the states to favor the amendment.)

But why did the mint select Paul, who was never a spouse to anyone, much less a president, and who spent much of her most active years *battling* presidents like Woodrow Wilson? The mint gave two reasons: she was "a leading strategist in the suffrage movement, who was instrumental in gaining

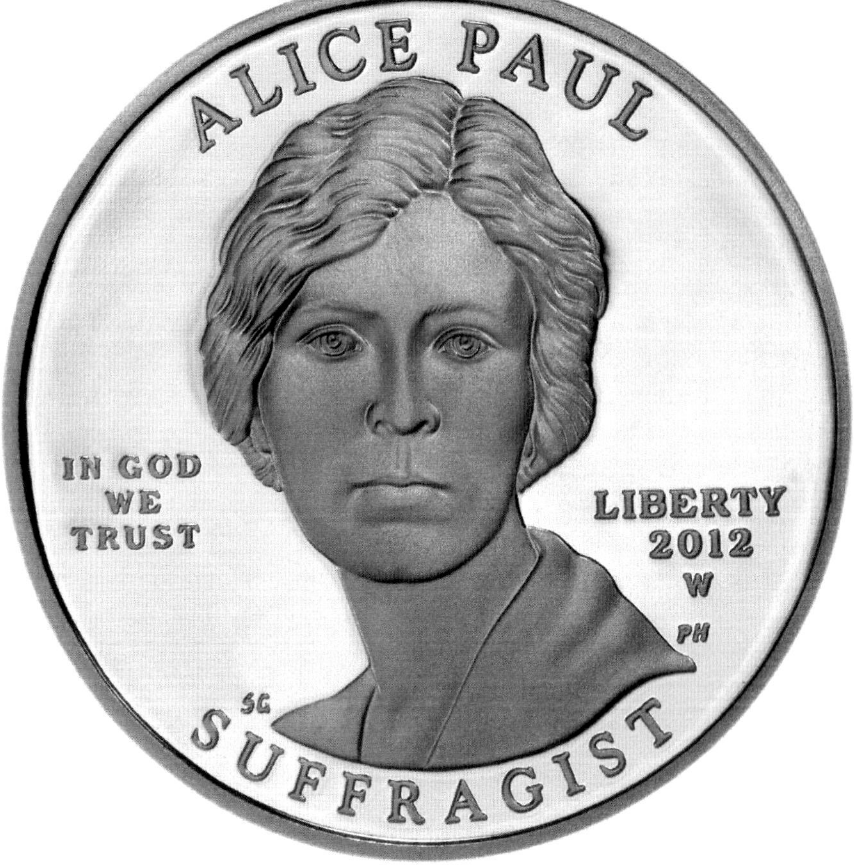

Alice Paul was honored on a $10 gold coin, issued by the U.S. Mint in 2012 and costing as much as $1,100 today. *U.S. Mint.*

women the right to vote upon the adoption of the 19th Amendment and thus the ability to participate in the election of future presidents." Reason two? She was born on January 11, 1885, during the term of President Arthur.

The front of the coin bears a likeness of her face and the reverse has an image of a woman marching in a suffrage parade, holding an American flag and wearing a banner reading, "Votes for Women." Roughly the same size as a quarter, the coin has a face value of ten dollars but has never sold for anything close to that since it's made of a half ounce of pure gold. Its opening price at the mint in 2012 was $1,054, but it eventually fell with the value of gold to $840 and then sold out. In 2015, you can find them selling for between $800 and $1,500, depending on condition and gold prices.

Paul had earlier been honored on a U.S. postage stamp. The seventy-eight-cent issue appeared in 1995. Why seventy-eight cents? That was the amount needed to mail a three-ounce letter and prompted a *Philadelphia Inquirer* writer to note an irony: "Paul was a diminutive little woman of 90 pounds, and she appears on a stamp that goes on oversized, overweight mail of the 3-ounce variety."

There were 100 million copies of her face printed on that stamp, while only thirteen thousand of the gold coins were issued. One wonders how Alice Paul would have felt about all this.

A PAIR OF PIONEERING HEALERS

Ridgefield has had more than its share of pioneering women, and among them, two of the nation's earliest female physicians. One was born in town, and the other lived and had deep roots here—and also had a rather troublesome father whom she hated.

By the end of the nineteenth century, female doctors represented only 5 percent of American physicians and numbered around seven thousand—today, nearly half of all new physicians are female. And 5 percent was a large portion, considering men's prejudices against female doctors. One of the most outspoken "authorities" against women studying in universities was Harvard professor Edward H. Clarke, who declared in 1874 that women seeking advanced education would develop "monstrous brains and puny bodies [and] abnormally weak digestion." With attitudes like that prevalent, most of the early female physicians were educated in female-only institutions.

Such was the case for Annie Keeler Bailey, who earned her medical degree from the Women's Medical College of New York Infirmary in 1885 and was probably the first woman to practice in Danbury and one of the first in Connecticut.

The Woman's Medical College of the New York Infirmary opened in 1868, with fifteen students and a faculty of nine. It was founded by Dr. Elizabeth Blackwell (1821–1910), a native of England who became the first woman to earn a medical degree in the United States (from Hobart College). She served as professor of hygiene, and her younger sister Emily, the third female doctor in America, was professor of obstetrics and diseases of women. The year after the college's opening, Elizabeth returned to England to establish a medical school in London, leaving the college in Emily's hands.

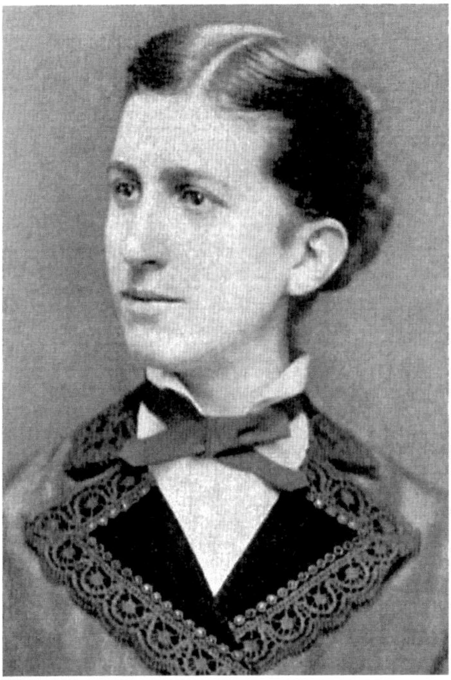

Annie Keeler Bailey, one of the first female physicians in Connecticut, began practicing in 1885. *From family archives.*

Having graduated from the State Normal School (now Central Connecticut University) in New Britain in 1876, Annie Keeler Bailey arrived at the Woman's Medical College in 1881. The school incorporated Dr. Elizabeth Blackwell's more modern ideas about medical education that included a four-year training period with much more extensive clinical training than had previously been required. The college, which wound up graduating 364 doctors, closed in 1899 when Cornell University promised to admit all the students attending the school. After graduating, Dr. Bailey spent a year at New York Infirmary, which specialized in treating women and children.

She opened a practice in Danbury in May 1886. Over the years, she lived in Danbury in what one observer called "a beautiful residence." She spent much of her childhood in Ridgefield with her mother at the family homestead in Ridgebury. She never married.

Over her career, she published a number of articles in medical journals. She was active in promoting nursing, and meetings of the Graduate Nurses' Association of Danbury Hospital were often held at her home.

Like Dr. Blackwell and like her mother, Dr. Bailey was deeply religious. Her opinions on the power of God to heal the sick were published in the *Women's Medical Journal* under the title "Faith and Works." She also delivered addresses on nonmedical religious subjects. In the 1890s, she spoke at the First Congregational Church in Danbury on biblical prophesies related to missionary work in Africa, a talk that was popular enough to be turned into a book, *Prophesies Fulfilled in History: The House of Israel*, published in 1895 by the Danbury Medical Printing Company. Modern reprints of it can be purchased today. So can copies of *Prophecies in Course of Fulfillment: The House of Judah*, another address-turned-book, published in 1896. Bailey's thoughts on religion were fairly widely quoted around the turn of the twentieth century and even appeared in the *Atlanta Constitution*, which called her "one of the best known woman physicians in Connecticut."

Bailey's mother was steeped in Ridgefield history. Emily Keeler Bailey was a daughter of Colonel Nehemiah Keeler and granddaughter of Lieutenant Nehemiah Keeler, who fought in the Revolution and operated a famous tavern and stagecoach stop just south of Ridgebury Cemetery.

Annie's father, Halcyon Gilbert Bailey, was apparently a ne'er-do-well and a bit of a character. He was born just across the state line on Dingle Ridge Road in North Salem. Sometime during the 1860s, he ran a satirical political campaign in Ridgefield, complete with posters, for the "office of hayward," a colonial-era official who apprehended and impounded errant livestock, especially pigs. The office had long been discontinued. Smithsonian historian Silvio Bedini, who has a short essay on Bailey in his *Ridgefield in Review*, describes the man as "noted for his mischievous disposition."

Emily Keeler Bailey didn't appreciate his carryings on, and by 1880, they were divorced. H.G. Bailey was by then living in New York City, working as a clerk in a store. He died in 1905 and is buried in the Peach Lake Cemetery in North Salem, New York, with other members of his Bailey family. Emily, who died in 1907, is buried in Ridgebury Cemetery under her maiden name with her daughter and a son who died young.

After both her parents died, Dr. Bailey successfully petitioned the Superior Court in Bridgeport to have her name changed to Annie Keeler, saying she wanted to "free the honor of her mother's family from the taint arising from the name of her father," according to a story that appeared in newspapers throughout the nation. "Father," she was quoted as saying, "was a man addicted to excessive dissipation, shocking immorality and profanity. He was a disgrace to the family."

For whatever reason, the story also pointed out that "Dr. Bailey wears her hair short."

Dr. Bailey died in 1927 of injuries sustained in an auto accident. She is buried with her mother and brother in Ridgebury Cemetery with a monument that, despite her court-approved name change, says "Annie Keeler Bailey M.D." However, in its obituary, the *Ridgefield Press* called her Dr. Annie Keeler. "There was an abundance of floral tributes, attesting to the esteem in which Dr. Keeler was held," the *Press* said in describing the funeral at the Ridgebury Congregational Church where Reverend Hugh

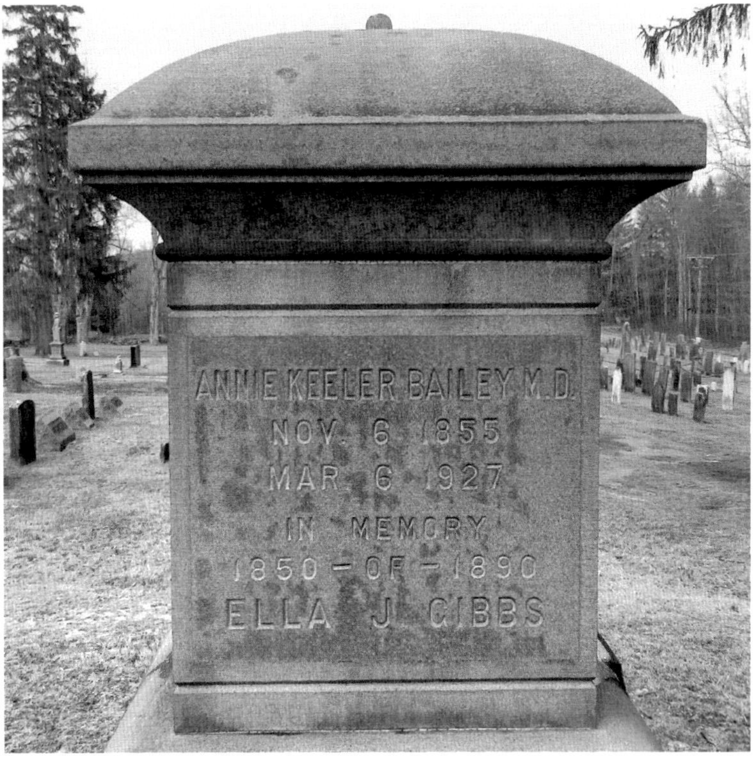

Although she adopted her mother's maiden name, Keeler, late in life because her father was abusive, Dr. Annie Keeler Bailey's gravestone has her full birth name. Ella Gibbs was probably a family friend. *Photograph by author.*

Shields "paid tribute to the public spirit of Dr. Keeler and to her character and medical ability."

Dr. Alice E. Rockwell did not have the paternal problems faced by Dr. Bailey. A Ridgefield native, she became one of the first women to practice medicine in Bridgeport, which is Connecticut's largest city.

Born in 1895, she was a daughter of Nathan and Emily Lounsbury Rockwell, descended from the family that produced the two Lounsbury governors, as well as early Ridgefield settlers. She studied at Wheaton College in Norton, Massachusetts, and Goucher College and earned her medical degree from Johns Hopkins.

After her graduation in 1921, the Rockefeller Foundation sent Dr. Rockwell to the Peking Medical Institute in China, where she interned and served as assistant resident in medicine. She returned to Ridgefield for a while, living in the family homestead on East Ridge, and then in 1932, she joined the staff of Bellevue Hospital in New York, specializing in pediatrics. Four years later, she opened her practice in Bridgeport, near Beardsley Park. She retired in 1959 and died in 1972 at the age of seventy-six.

SANTA ASHBEE'S MANY FRIENDS

Retirees, too, had their place in Ridgefield history. When Charles F. Ashbee died in 1962, the front page of the May 31 issue of the *Ridgefield Press* announced: "C.F. Ashbee, Santa Claus, Dies at 89."

By then, Charley Ashbee, a retired insurance executive, had become a local legend. "Mr. Ashbee spent nearly as much of his long life portraying Santa Claus and delighting the children of this town as he devoted to the insurance business," the *Ridgefield Press* said in his obituary. "Donning a Santa Claus suit became a habit with Uncle Charley soon after he and Mrs. Ashbee settled here."

Ashbee was born in New York City in 1872 and moved to Wilton Road West around 1929. Soon after, he began his Santa service when he pinch-hit for someone who was unable to act at a church school party. He took on other appearances and, by the early 1930s, had already become a fixture at Christmas celebrations on Main Street and with various organizations. Over the more than thirty years that he played the role, he wore out three Santa suits and three sets of wigs and whiskers.

"Charley got to be such an important part of the Christmas season that letters addressed to the man at the North Pole were rerouted to him," reported Dick Venus, a former postmaster who was also the first town historian. "He would never fail to visit the home of the little kid that wrote the letter." Venus added, "In many cases, he was able to locate a toy that a youngster had asked for. When he did, he would take it along with him and leave it with the parents, to be put under the tree. Not only the kids, but grownups as well, thought that he was just the greatest."

For all the joy he gave children, he was named Rotary Citizen of the Year in 1960. A year later, when he was about eighty-eight, Ashbee missed his first Christmas as Santa in three decades. He was seriously ill and confined to the Altnacraig nursing home. Scores of the town's children went to Altnacraig to visit him that Christmas season; some knew he was the person who had played Santa in the past while to others he was just a nice man. He died in the spring.

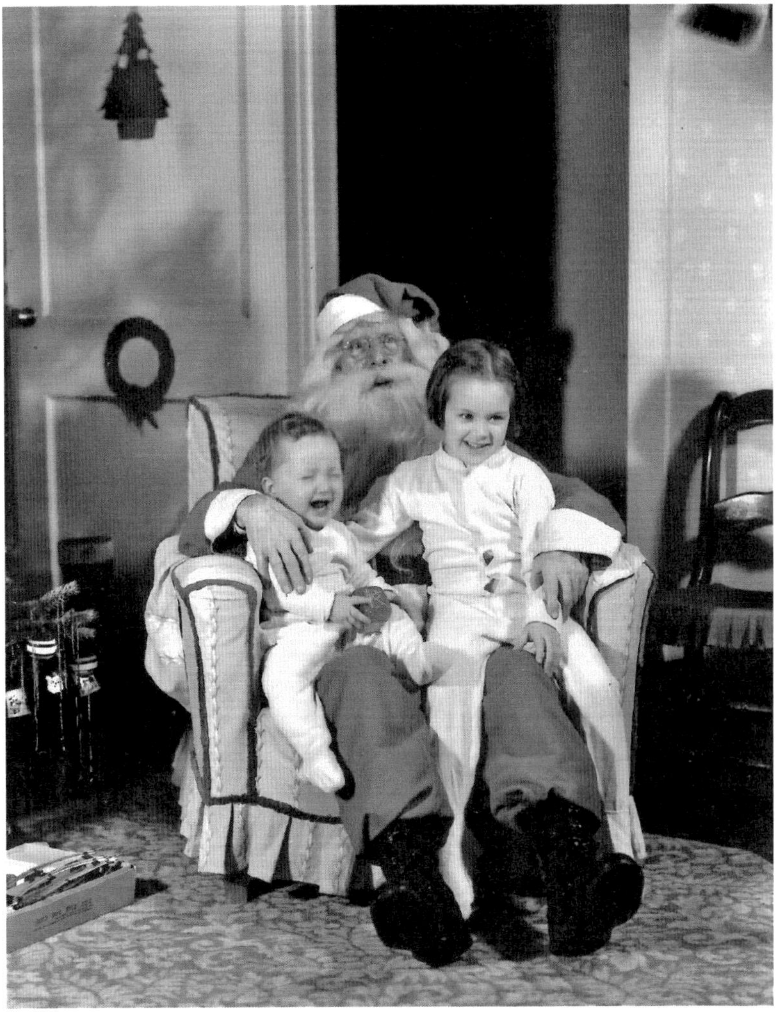

Charley Ashbee is shown here in the 1940s or 1950s with two unidentified children—one perhaps a tad too young to appreciate his talents at Santa Clausing. *Courtesy of the Ridgefield Historical Society.*

Incidentally, among Ashbee's off-season hobbies was autograph collecting, and he had the signatures of every president except George Washington. He also collected signatures of Civil War generals and had all but J.E.B. Stuart and Stonewall Jackson.

Everett Lounsbury Jr., who developed Ashbee Lane off Route 7 in the 1960s, named the road the year after Charley died. Lounsbury was undoubtedly a Santa fan, one of thousands in Ridgefield.

LOWLY WORM ON A RIDGEFIELD FARM

The man who created Bananas Gorilla with his armload of watches, Sergeant Murphy blowing his whistle and Mr. Fixit with his chest of tools, was—when he was less famous—a Ridgefielder.

Countless kids who grew up from the 1960s onward have known the creations of Richard Scarry, including the particularly popular Huckle Cat and Lowly Worm. "Scarry revealed to kids that the everyday world was a place that could be understood—and that learning was fun," said one biographer of the author and illustrator.

Born in 1919 in Boston, Richard McClure Scarry dropped out of business school and then studied at the Museum of Fine Arts School in Boston. After serving as an army lieutenant during World War II, he became a freelance artist in New York City. In 1950, he illustrated Katherine Jackson's *The Animals Merry Christmas* for Simon & Schuster, and a career was born. First editions of this nineteen-cent book can fetch hundreds of dollars today.

In February 1951, he and his wife, Patsy, moved to Ridgefield from New York City, leasing a place on the Conklin farm on North Street, a locale that inspired many of his later farming illustrations. In 1953, the couple bought their first home, also on North Street. The Scarrys could often be seen driving around town in their distinctive MG sports car.

In 1958, when Ridgefield was celebrating its 250th anniversary, Scarry drew a lively and entertaining map of the route of the British troops as they marched through—and camped in—Ridgefield at the time of the Battle of Ridgefield. It appeared in Silvio Bedini's history, *Ridgefield in Review*, published in connection with the anniversary.

Throughout the 1950s, Scarry illustrated books for Golden Press. In 1955, he did Jane Werner's *Smokey the Bear*, a Golden Book. Many of today's images of Smokey the Bear are based on how Scarry imagined and drew him, though the fictional character had been drawn on posters since the early 1940s.

In 1953, the Scarrys' son was born. Though they named him Richard Jr., he was always called Huck—like the Busytown cat that would follow—and today, Huck Scarry produces children's books himself.

In 1959, the Scarrys moved to Westport and ten years later to Switzerland.

Richard Scarry's first major success as an author-illustrator was *The Best Word Book Ever*, published in 1963, which introduced Busytown, a village full of his now famous characters. In a 2002 compilation of the bestselling children's books of all time, it was ranked twenty-seventh, with 3.9 million

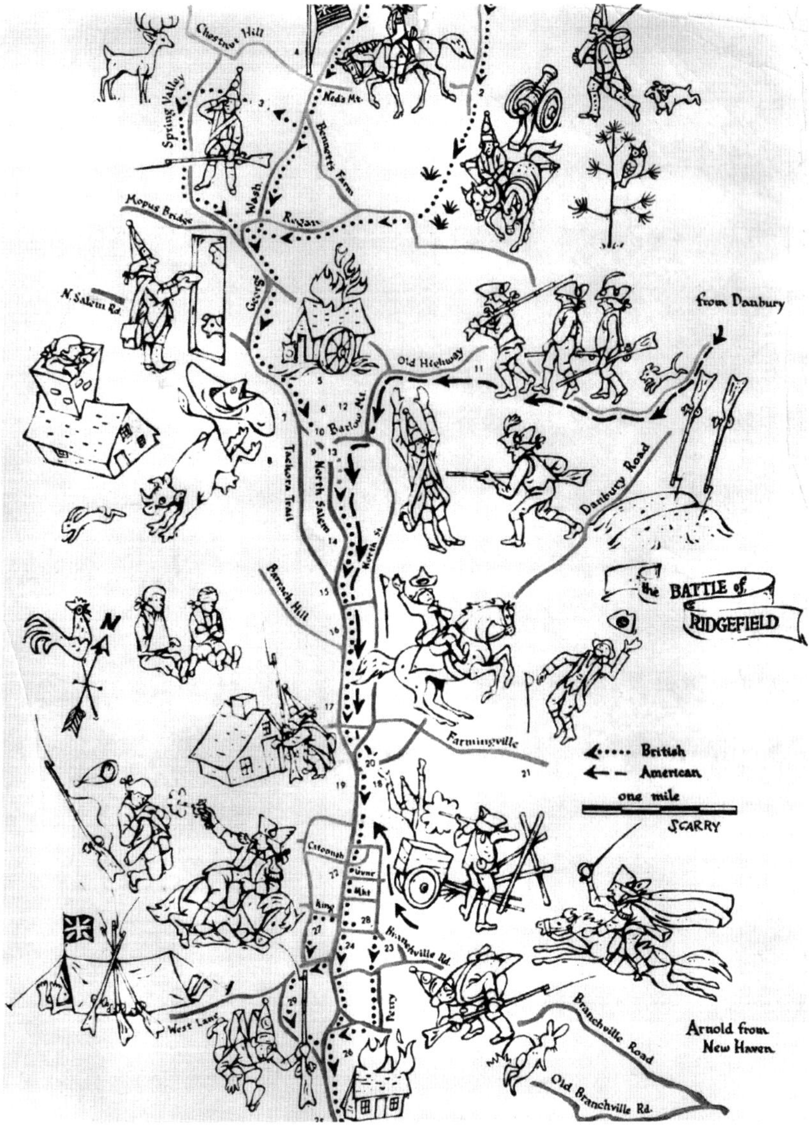

Richard Scarry, creator of Busytown, drew this map in 1958 for Ridgefield's celebration of its 250th anniversary. It appeared in Silvio Bedini's book *Ridgefield in Review*. *From the* Ridgefield Press *archives.*

copies sold. And considering that Dr. Seuss and Harry Potter books made up nearly half the titles ahead of it, that's a good showing. Over his twenty-six-year career, Scarry did more than three hundred books that have sold more than 100 million copies in thirty languages; scores of them are still in print.

"I'm not interested in creating a book that is read once and then placed on the shelf and forgotten," he once said. "I am very happy when people write that they have worn out my books, or that they are held together by Scotch tape. I consider that the ultimate compliment."

Richard Scarry died in 1994 in Switzerland at the age of seventy-five—his papers and much of his art are now in the University of Connecticut archives. And Huck, at last word, is living and working in Vienna.

SUPERMAN'S MAN

While Lowly Worm may have had his beginnings in Ridgefield, Superman also spent time here. If you were among the many fans of the Man of Steel between 1940 and the 1960s, you saw the artistry of Wayne Boring, a Ridgefield cartoonist who brought Superman to life for millions who read the newspaper "funny pages."

"Comics legend Wayne Boring played a major role in visually defining the most well-known superhero in the world during the peak of Superman's popularity," wrote comics historian Michael Vance.

Born in 1916 in Minneapolis, Boring studied at the Chicago

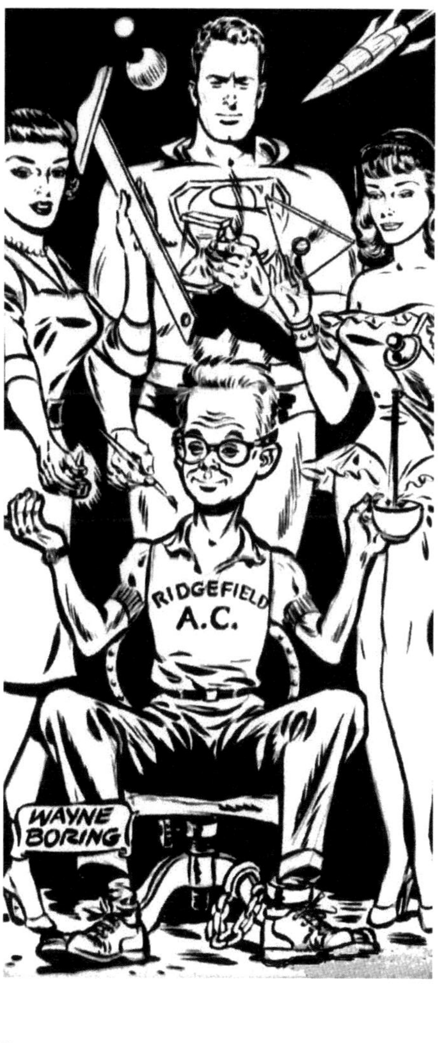

Wayne Boring drew this "self-portrait," showing Superman, Lois Lane and a friend supplying the tools of his trade, including coffee. Notice his left ankle is chained to the chair. His drawing was used in a promotion for the Ridgefield Athletic Club in 1960. *From the* Ridgefield Press *archives.*

Art Institute, where he took a drawing course under J. Allen St. John, the then famous illustrator of the Tarzan books, to learn how to produce the muscular, Tarzan-like figure.

In 1940, after a stint as a newspaper illustrator and some freelance comics work, he was hired to help illustrate the new but growing *Superman* strip, started in 1938 by Joe Shuster and Jerry Siegel. At first he "ghosted" strips, filling in bodies after Shuster drew the faces. By the mid-1940s, he was the sole comics illustrator and by 1965 had drawn more than 1,350 Sunday and 8,300 daily *Superman* strips, as well as illustrated many of the comic books. In all of those strips and books, incidentally, he never once drew Superman changing into costume in a phone booth, a TV series gimmick that always annoyed Boring.

In 1957, he moved to Lincoln Lane in Ridgefield. Ten years later, DC Comics started cutting costs and dismissed several of its veteran artists, including Boring. After that, he drew backgrounds for the Prince Valiant series by Hal Foster, who lived in Redding, until 1972. He also drew for Marvel comics on and off, but late in life, after moving to Florida, he worked as a bank security guard to make ends meet. He died in 1982 in Florida.

Today, originals of *Superman* strips drawn by Boring bring as much as $11,000 at auction.

"Wayne Boring's *Superman* is one of the most enduring characters in the comics hobby," comics art historian Richard Halegua has written. "Boring's stylized artwork and fine linework along with his ability to handle science fiction subjects has made him one of the most popular artists of his time, and among the most remembered in comics history."

THE HISTORIAN WHO LOVED RIDGEFIELD

For a small town, Ridgefield has had a wealth of historians, with no fewer than three full-sized histories written about it, plus many shorter works. One of those brief histories was penned by one of the nation's most prominent historians, a rare winner of *two* Pulitzer Prizes for historical writing.

Allan Nevins was still a young man when he came to Ridgefield in the 1920s, perhaps to work on a thesis in graduate school or to complete one of his early books on journalism. He lived at the Elms Inn and was so taken by the town that he wrote a fifty-page profile, published by the Elms as a booklet entitled *An Historical Sketch of Ridgefield*. While the book is undated, it was one of the first written by Nevins, who went on to complete fifty volumes of history and biography, including the acclaimed eight-volume story of the Civil War, called *Ordeal of the Union.*

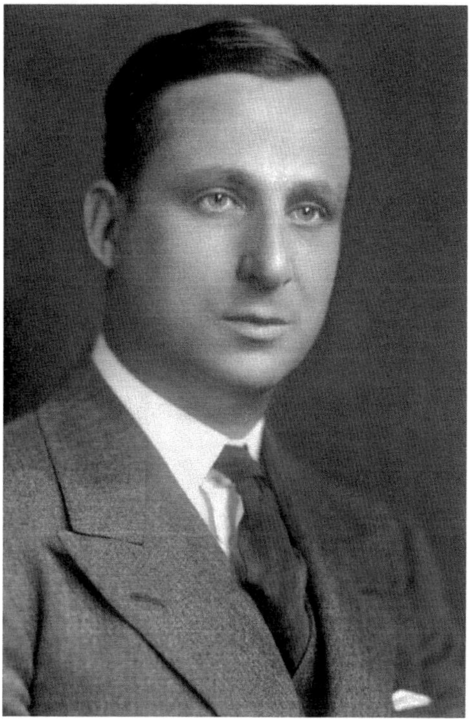

Pulitzer Prize–winning historian Allan Nevins wrote two paeans to Ridgefield and its history. *Courtesy of Columbia University.*

Born on an Illinois farm in 1890, Nevins earned bachelor's and master's degrees in English at the University of Illinois and then moved to New York City, where he became a reporter for the *New York Evening Post.* That job inspired one of his first books. Combining his work with his love of history, it was called *The* Evening Post*: A Century of Journalism* and was published in 1922. He might have been working on *The American States During and After the Revolution, 1775–1789*, published in 1929, when he was living in Ridgefield. Or perhaps his time here inspired that book.

His historical research and writings led to an appointment in 1928 to the history faculty at Columbia University, where he remained until his retirement in 1958. He then moved to California and continued to write; he was still working on his Civil War series when he died in 1971. His biographies *Grover Cleveland: A Study in Courage* (1933) and *Hamilton Fish: The Inner History of the Grant Administration* (1936) each won a Pulitzer.

Professor Nevins was a friend and supporter of John F. Kennedy and wrote the foreword to Kennedy's *Profiles in Courage.* He also wrote the foreword to Silvio Bedini's 1958 history of the town, *Ridgefield in Review*, in which Nevins sings Ridgefield's praises like a chamber of commerce director:

> *When I made acquaintance with Ridgefield some three decades ago, it delighted me for several reasons. The chief was that it made an ideal center for long country walks, as picturesque as those from a Cotswold*

> *or Burgundian village, and a good deal wilder...Ridgefield is set in a remarkably diversified terrain of hills, streams and woods, where no factory smoke stains the sky, and the distant train whistle seldom interrupts the cawing crows.*
>
> *My second reason for taking pleasure in the place lay in its historic memories. For it cherishes and fittingly exhibits its relics of colonial and Revolutionary days. Perhaps this filiopietistic trait has developed because Ridgefield has grown and changed but slowly. As a third reason for delight in the place, I liked its neat elegance. It is not merely shining and well improved; it has a distinct and old-fashioned gentility. Finally, it seemed to me a remarkably successful amalgam of new and old, of the provincial and the cosmopolitan.*

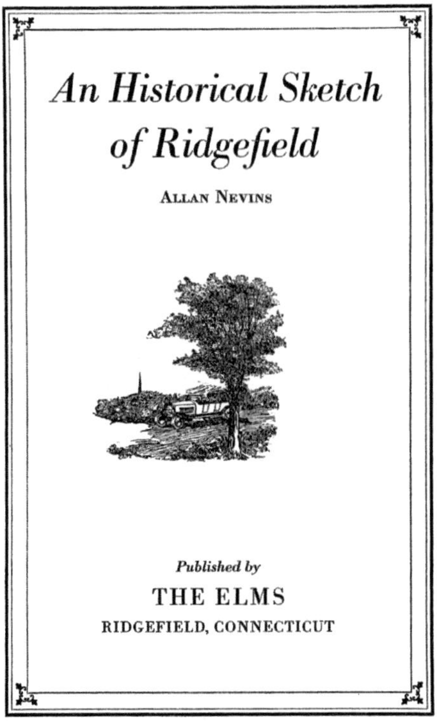

An Historical Sketch of Ridgefield

ALLAN NEVINS

Published by

THE ELMS

RIDGEFIELD, CONNECTICUT

Allan Nevin's historical essay on Ridgefield was published in the 1920s before the author won two Pulitzer Prizes for his biographies. This is the title page. *From the author's collection, thanks to Rudy Ruggles.*

Bedini, incidentally, was no amateur historian himself. A Ridgefield native who became a curator at the Smithsonian Institution in Washington, he went on to write more than twenty books of history after completing *Ridgefield in Review*, his first book, in only three months. Perhaps a bit of his inspiration came from Professor Nevins, who was teaching at Columbia while Bedini was a student there before World War II.

HAWTHORNE'S HELPER

Another historian who loved Ridgefield was a remarkable writer long before there were Pulitzer Prizes to be won.

Samuel G. Goodrich was an extraordinary fellow on several fronts. The man who was known to millions in the nineteenth century as "Peter Parley" provided the nation with a new kind of textbook for its schools, gave Ridgefield a remarkable account of life in the town more than two hundred years ago and helped introduce the world to one of American's greatest authors.

Samuel Griswold Goodrich was born in 1793 in a house, no longer standing, near the corner of West and Golf Lanes. His father, Reverend S.G. Goodrich, had moved there in 1789 to become the third minister of the First Congregational Church. When young Samuel was four, his father had a new home built on four acres on High Ridge. (The house still stands today at the head of Parley Lane.) Samuel spent his childhood there and left in 1808 to work in a Danbury store and then in Hartford, eventually winding up in the publishing field in Boston.

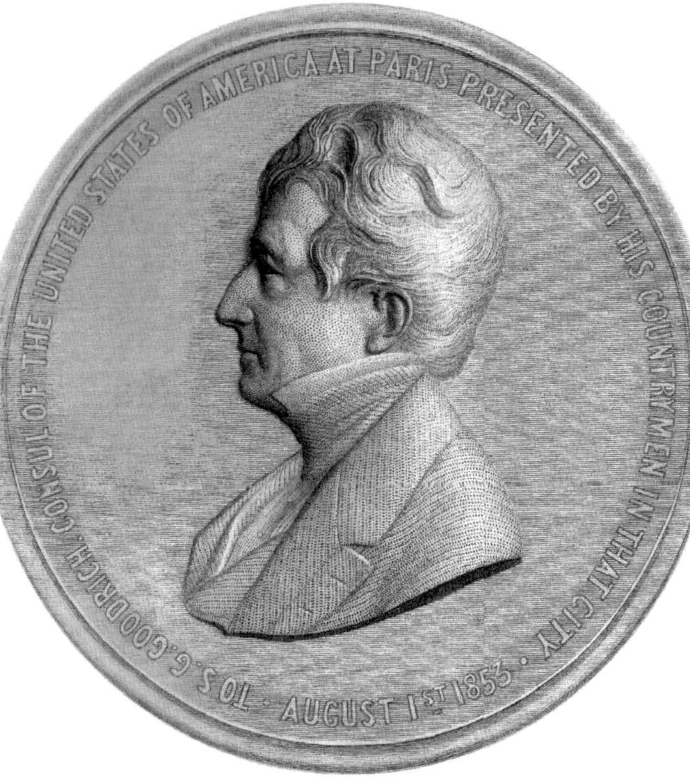

Samuel G. Goodrich's profile as it was shown on a medal presented to him in 1853 in honor of his service as U.S. consul in Paris. *From* Recollections of a Lifetime.

Literally millions of his Peter Parley books—chiefly histories, biographies and geographies—were sold in the 1800s. Some scholars consider Goodrich to be the father of the modern textbook because he made his schoolbooks interesting to children, both in the way they were written and in the way they were illustrated.

His brother, Charles A. Goodrich, was also an author whose histories were widely used in nineteenth-century schools. Charles was a Yale graduate. Samuel never went to college, and when asked where he was schooled, he would respond, "at West Lane," referring to the one-room Ridgefield schoolhouse he had attended as a boy. "Generally speaking, this has ended the inquiry, whether because my interlocutors have confounded this venerable institution with 'Lane Seminary,' or have not thought it worthwhile to risk an exposure of their ignorance as to the college in which I was educated, I am unable to say."

Those words appeared in his 1,100-page *Recollections of a Lifetime*, published four years before his death in 1860. This autobiography offers more than 200 pages on what it was like growing up in Ridgefield at the turn of the nineteenth century and is a unique look at the life and characters in the town then. Few communities in this country are fortunate enough to have as extensive and as intimate a report on daily life two centuries ago.

Historian Allan Nevins, who called Goodrich "Ridgefield's greatest literary son," said his "greatest service to pure literature" was not his books but his illustrated annual, *The Token*, which he edited from 1828 until 1842. *The Token* published the works of rising authors, including Henry Wadsworth Longfellow, Nathaniel Hawthorne, Edward Everett, John Adams and Horace Greeley, as well as Goodrich himself. Hawthorne called *The Token* "a sort of hothouse, where native flowers were made to bloom like exotics." During this period, these annuals became so popular that they were widely pirated, and Goodrich became what Nevins called "a figure of importance in the literary world." Hawthorne, no doubt with tongue in cheek, called Goodrich "a gentleman of many excellent qualities, although a publisher."

Nevins maintained that "Hawthorne…owed Goodrich a heavy debt, which he frankly acknowledged, for encouragement while he was still totally unknown. Goodrich saw the romancer's first sketches when they were published anonymously, and inquired concerning their authorship, thus bringing about a correspondence."

In those letters, Goodrich found Hawthorne depressed because his early works were not being published or appreciated. "I combated his despondency, and assured him of triumph, if he would persevere in a literary career," Goodrich wrote in *Recollections*.

Goodrich not only published but also promoted Hawthorne, writing essays for newspapers that praised his writing and networking on Hawthorne's behalf in the publishing world. "In 1837, he urged Hawthorne to publish a volume, and helped him find a firm to issue *Twice-Told Tales*," Nevins said.

Twice-Told Tales wound up getting fine reviews, including one from Edgar Allan Poe, who wrote: "The style of Hawthorne is purity itself. His tone is singularly effective—wild, plaintive, thoughtful, and in full accordance with his themes...We look upon him as one of the few men of indisputable genius to whom our country has as yet given birth." The Grolier Club, the nation's oldest society for book lovers, named *Twice-Told Tales* the most influential book of 1837.

Hawthorne went on to become famous for such novels as *The Scarlet Letter* and *The House of the Seven Gables* while Goodrich, by his own accounting, published more than 170 books under the name of Peter Parley. His last effort, which appeared in 1859, was a 1,400-page, two-volume tome, *The Animal Kingdom Illustrated*, also later called *Johnson's Natural History*. One of its more than 1,500 illustrations appears in this book.

Late in life, Goodrich was named U.S. consul in Paris, and although millions copies of his books were already in print, he took the opportunity to get some of his titles published in French. He may have been a literary man, but he was also a savvy businessman.

3

The Way We Were

Grog-Drinkers and Brandy Tipplers

Ridgefield today is a town of almost innumerable places to buy alcoholic beverages—be it from a shelf, a bar or a waitperson. But for much of its history, this was a "dry" community as far as the business of booze was concerned, and sales of alcohol were illegal. However, that didn't mean folks weren't tippling their homebrew—or illicitly bought spirits.

For better or worse, alcohol has long been a part of Ridgefield life. The chief drink back in the 1700s and 1800s was cider—not the sweet stuff of today's grocery stores but aged and alcoholic concoctions produced at cider mills or in backyard stills. According to Samuel G. Goodrich ("Peter Parley"), writing about the early 1800s, "Cider was the universal table beverage. Cider brandy and whisky were soon after evoked from the infernal caldron of evil spirits. I remember, in my boyhood, to have seen a strange, zigzag tin tube, denominated a 'still,' belonging to one of our neighbors, converting, drop by drop, certain innocent liquids into the infernal fire-water." Ridgefield today has a Still Road, recalling the distillery that Hull Keeler operated thereabouts in the 1870s. According to Silvio Bedini, this distillery produced cider brandy.

Goodrich also reported that rum was popular in town in the eighteenth and early nineteenth centuries. "A half-pint of it was given as a matter of course to every day laborer, more particularly in the summer season," he wrote. "In all families, rich or poor, it was offered to male visitors as an essential point of hospitality, or even good manners."

Women, he said, "took their schnapps, then named 'Hopkins' Elixir,' which was the most delicious and seductive means of getting tipsy that has been invented." Even "crying babies were silenced with hot toddy, then esteemed an infallible remedy for wind on the stomach." He added, "Every man imbibed his morning dram, and this was esteemed temperance."

His father, Reverend S.G. Goodrich, seemed displeased with the drinking that was going on in 1800, when he penned a report on the community. "We had the last year not more than five taverns in town," he said. That might seem like bad news—and, indeed, Ridgefield then had more taverns than churches (with only three of the latter). However, Goodrich added, "In years past we have had double that number [of taverns]."

He also maintained that the taverns were "not much frequented by the inhabitants of the town." It seems that "the grog-drinkers and brandy tipplers have found a way to be supplied at a cheaper rate than they can obtain at licensed inns."

"It is necessary that they should be prudent," he warned.

Even the town government paid for the distribution of alcohol. When the selectmen sponsored a large "celebration" on July 4, 1813, to support the War of 1812 effort, the event included patriotic readings, a military demonstration, music and rum. Expenses billed to the town included $18.25 for a keg of powder, $1.00 for ten pounds of cheese and $1.09 for three and a half quarts of rum.

Despite Reverend Goodrich's report on taverns, they were major social gathering places in the early nineteenth century. Ridgebury at one point had three watering holes while Main Street had at least two: the Smith Tavern, where the library now stands, and the Keeler Tavern, today a museum.

The Smith family may have opened its first tavern at Main and Prospect Streets by 1719, when an old ledger records alcoholic payments, such as those of Amos Whittmor, who in 1719 consumed many "pots of sider [*sic*] at diverse times," often with "pots of rum," according to an 1890s profile of the Smith Tavern. Just before the tavern was torn down to make way for the library, the profile said, "in a tiny cupboard underneath the stairs are still shown the shelves for holding bottles, cups, and tankards, with which the jovial souls of Ridgefield might make merry."

"The tavern of those days was generally the center of news, and the gathering place for balls, musical entertainments, public shows, &c.," wrote Samuel G. Goodrich in his *Recollections of a Lifetime*. The Keeler Tavern, he added, "had special claims to notice. It was, in the first place, on the great thoroughfare of that day, between Boston and New York, and had become

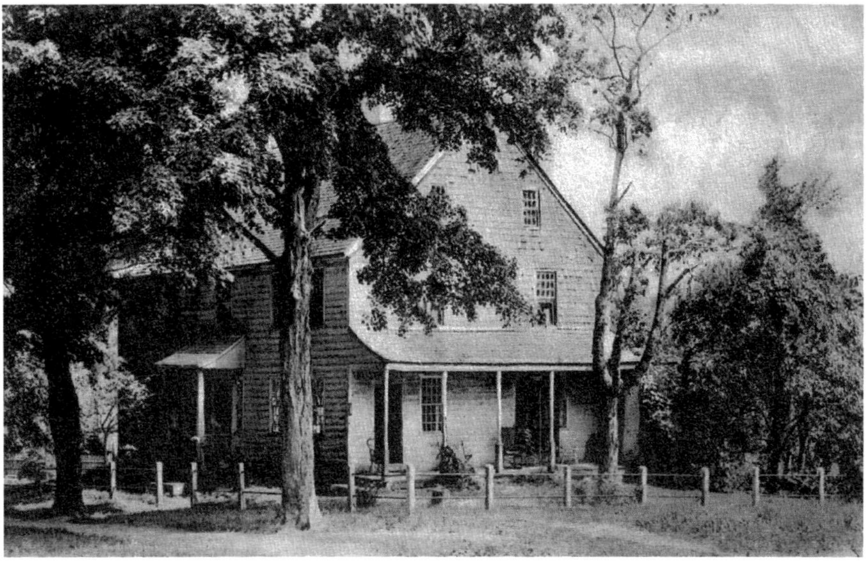

The Smith Tavern operated throughout the nineteenth century on the site of the current Ridgefield Library. *From the* Ridgefield Press *archives.*

a general and favorite stopping-place for travelers. It was, moreover, kept by a hearty old gentleman, who united in his single person the varied functions of publican, postmaster, representative, justice of the peace, and I know not what else. He besides had a thrifty wife, whose praise was in all the land."

Tavern types were probably not far different then than now and included mischievous pranksters. One of Ridgefield's best-known nineteenth-century wits was Matthew Olmstead of Olmstead Lane, who specialized in building stonewalls and frequented the Keeler Tavern. Author Goodrich tells of the kind of fun he liked to have:

> *On a cold stormy day in December—as I received the tale—a man chanced to come into the bar-room of Keeler's tavern, where Mat Olmstead and several of his companions were lounging. The stranger had on a new hat of the latest fashion, and still shining with the gloss of the iron. He seemed conscious of his dignity, and carried his head in such a manner as to invite attention to it. Mat's knowing eye immediately detected the weakness of the stranger; so he approached him, and said—*
>
> *"What a very nice hat you've got on. Pray who made it?"*
>
> *"Oh, it came from New York," was the reply.*
>
> *"Well, let me take it," said Mat.*

> *The stranger took it off his head, gingerly, and handed it to him.*
> *"It is a wonderful nice hat," said Matthew; "and I see it's a real salamander!"*
> *"Salamander?" said the other. "What's that?"*
> *"Why a real salamander hat won't burn!"*
> *"No? I never heard of that before: I don't believe it's one of that kind."*
> *"Sartain sure; I'll bet you a mug of flip of it."*
> *"Well, I'll stand you!"*
> *"Done: now I'll just put it under the fore-stick?"*
> *It being thus arranged, Mat put the hat under the fore-stick into a glowing mass of coals. In an instant it took fire, collapsed, and rolled into a black, crumpled mass of cinders.*
> *"I du declare," said Mat Olmstead, affecting great astonishment, "it ain't a salamander hat arter all. Well; I'll pay the flip!"*

"Flip," incidentally, was a sort of rum-based eggnog.

The town had at least two manufacturers of alcoholic beverages. Hezekiah Scott, known as "Uncle Kiah," produced cider at a mill in the Scotland District (Kiah's Brook along Ledges Road was named for him). And Hull Keeler specialized in cider brandy.

Alcohol, of course, was not without its problems. Until 1875, there were no newspapers in Ridgefield to report on drunken brawls or alcoholic fathers abandoning their families, but such incidents were occurring. Anna Marie

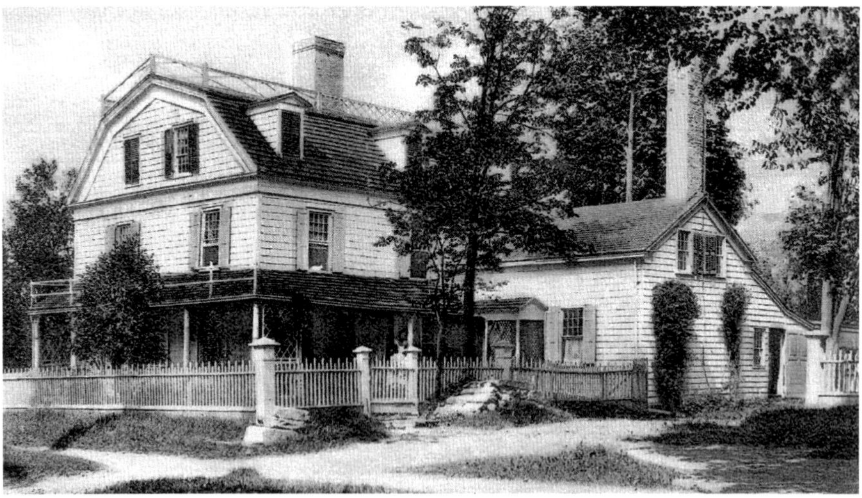

Keeler Tavern was an inn, a post office, a meeting place and, of course, a local pub. Here, Matthew Olmstead played his tricks on unwary visitors. *Postcard from author's collection.*

Resseguie of the Keeler Tavern mentioned two alcohol-related deaths. Five days before Christmas 1851, "a Mr. Riggs was frozen to death, being as supposed at the time intoxicated. He was found on Tuesday morning, having crawled out of the path, stretched himself on his back, and folded his arms." On November 26, 1852, the day after Thanksgiving, she notes: "Today the bell tolled for Mr. Eben Gilbert, found dead in a ditch, lying with face downward, his bottle by his side."

By this time, temperance movements were well underway in the country and in town. In 1854, Reverend Clinton Clark preached a strong temperance sermon at the First Congregational Church, calling for a Prohibition Law and maintaining that the only time strong drink is appropriate is "to him that is ready to perish."

In 1872, a new state law allowed towns to ban liquor sales. That August, forty people petitioned the selectmen for a town meeting to consider "the propriety of instructing the Select Men not to recommend any person to be licensed to sell liquors in the Town of Ridgefield." They believed "the sale and use of a beverage of intoxicating liquors is a great curse of any community, productive of much of the crime and misery which affects society." Signers included many prominent citizens.

It was the beginning of a protracted battle that lasted forty years.

On September 3, 1872, a town meeting voted 104 to 49 to ban the sale of intoxicating liquors in Ridgefield. The vote was soon thrown out because the state law allowing local option did not go into effect until September 15, twelve days after the Ridgefield vote. So prohibitionists launched a second petition drive. On September 28, a second town meeting was held on banning liquor sales, but only thirty-two people showed up. The meeting adjourned and met again on October 7, when a ban was finally passed again.

By April 1873, some Ridgefielders were getting thirsty. Twenty-five men—including Gould Rockwell, who had signed a previous petition to ban liquor sales—turned in a petition to rescind the "no license" vote of October 7, 1872. Signers include Peter P. Cornen, an oil baron and probably the town's first millionaire, and Lewis H. Bailey, prominent businessman who built Bailey Avenue and who owned a local hotel.

On April 26, 1873, at probably one of the most "spirited" town meetings in Ridgefield history, voters were asked to rescind the ban on liquor sales. George Lounsbury, later governor of Connecticut, moved that the selectmen be allowed to license the sale of "spirituous and intoxicating liquors, ale and lager beer." Up stood Phineas Lounsbury, George's brother and also a future governor. Unlike George, Phineas was a leader in the temperance movement.

He moved that the vote be taken by paper ballot and that the voting box be kept open for two hours, presumably to allow him to run up and down the village street to gather supporters. When the ballots were counted, 104 favored alcohol sales, and 111 opposed them. Ridgefield remained dry.

However, that December, the anti-alcohol forces discovered something defective about the previous votes to ban liquor sales and petitioned a fourth town meeting on the subject, warning that the previous three votes "are of doubtful validity and may be the cause of expensive litigation." And on December 20, 1873, drinkers won a round. A town meeting rescinded the previous alcohol sales ban but also voted against a new ban. It was close: a total of 136 people favored licensing and 131 were against.

Shocked at their defeat, prohibitionists took only two days to turn in yet another petition, calling for a fifth town meeting on the issue. Among the 25 signers were Reverend Daniel W. Teller, the minister of the First Congregational Church who would soon write the town's first history in book form; D. Crosby Baxter, who would found the *Ridgefield Press* in two years; and future governor Phineas Lounsbury. In January 1874, in three hours of balloting, the town meeting voted 152 to 129 not to license liquor sales.

The licensing question continued to be brought up at annual town meetings for many years. In 1874, the vote was 136 to 67 against licensing; in 1875, 136 to 69; and in 1876, 136 to 2. The movement was also getting some formal support. In 1882, the Ridgefield Division of the Sons of Temperance was formed.

There were ways to get alcohol legally. In 1877, the *Press* was carrying advertisements for Bininger's Old London Dock Gin, which was touted as being "especially designed for the use of the medical profession." This gin was "indispensable for females," the ad said, explaining that it was "good for nervousness, liver and kidney complaints. A delicious tonic."

The fact that alcohol sales were banned didn't stop the less law-abiding citizens from making some money—and getting in trouble. In April 1887, Henry Mead, William Crofut, Eugene Keeler and Mrs. F.B. Daniels—all members of prominent local families—were arrested and charged with several counts of illegal liquor sales. In town court, Mead bargained a fine of thirty dollars plus costs on one count. Daniels and Keeler were found guilty and fined thirty-five and thirty dollars, respectively; both said they would appeal to the Superior Court. Crofut was "let off with costs." "Probably no crusade against illicit liquor-selling has created such agitation of the public mind in this town," the *Press* said of the cases.

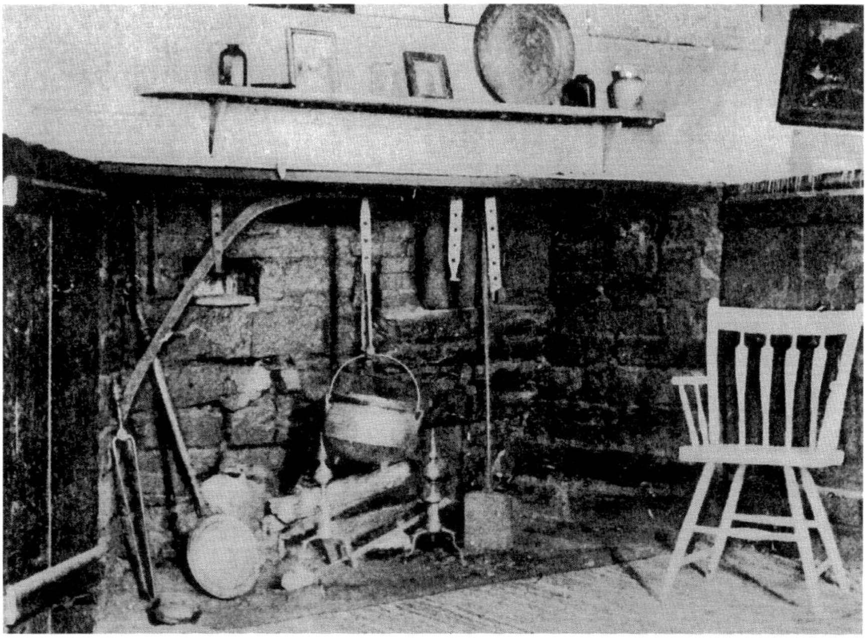

Many a Ridgefielder sat before the fire in the dining room of Landlord Smith's Tavern at Main and Prospect Streets, but for part of the nineteenth century, they weren't sipping grog or toddies, legally at least. *Postcard in author's collect.*

After years of meetings voting down the sale of alcohol in town, the annual town meeting in October 1890 voted to allow licenses by a close 132–23 margin, but the supporters of temperance rallied their forces to reinstate the ban one year later by the biggest margin ever recorded in the many votes on the issue: 296 to 56,

While taverns couldn't sell liquor, mobile stands were apparently doing it by 1896, when the annual town meeting included a resolution to "instruct the selectmen or other town officers to take measures to suppress the beer traffic in town from wagons coming from other towns." The voters decided "that the selectmen...are instructed to prohibit the sale of intoxicating liquors, ale, and lager beer from wagons or other vehicles, if it is possible to do so."

Despite the bans, drinking problems continued. Reverend Horace W. Byrnes told local Methodists in 1902 that he found empty liquor bottles behind the church, consumed perhaps by "husbands blighting the lives of their wives and blasting the future of their children" or by "boys who were breaking mothers' hearts and bringing fathers' gray heads in sorrow to the grave."

In 1909, the selectmen received yet another petition to allow liquor sales. They didn't like it and used town funds to pay to print it in full in the *Press*, "believing that the public would like to know the names of the voters who desire to introduce the saloon in our quiet village." Those "pro-saloon" signers included C.D. Crouchley, son of one of the selectmen; Hiram K. Scott Jr., whose father had been a prohibitionist judge; and H.D. Hull, father of future first selectman Harry E. Hull. When the vote was taken, Ridgefield remained dry, 194 for licensing and 204 opposed.

Finally, a couple years later, the town began allowing liquor sales. But for tipplers, the long-sought freedom didn't last long. In January 1919, the Eighteenth Amendment—enacting Prohibition—was ratified and took effect a year later. Connecticut was among the states that did not vote for ratification.

WHEN THE PIKE TURNED

While prohibition had prompted controversy in the past, tolls may be more apt to stir debate today as a system much hated by motorists. Tolls, though, were once considered a creative solution to improving transportation and communication in the region and in the state.

Two centuries ago, toll roads were called turnpikes. Fees were collected at a tollhouse, in front of which usually stood a long pole, or "pike," mounted on a post or style. The pike blocked passage until the toll was paid, whereupon the tollhouse keeper turned the pike to open the road.

In the early nineteenth century, Ridgefield had no fewer than three turnpike roads—and almost had a "plank road" to boot.

Turnpikes began to appear in this country in the 1790s as the need for better highways to connect towns and states became evident. The former colonies had broken ties with England and needed to manufacture more and more items that had once been imported. At the same time, the industrial age was just dawning; the nation sorely needed routes for raw materials and finished products to be transported as well as for people to travel in reasonable comfort.

Most post-Revolution intercity roads were terrible. Upkeep was often left to the people who owned property along them, and as a result many stretches were poorly maintained. Bridges were needed and drainage had to be taken care of; both were expensive and strained the budgets of many small towns

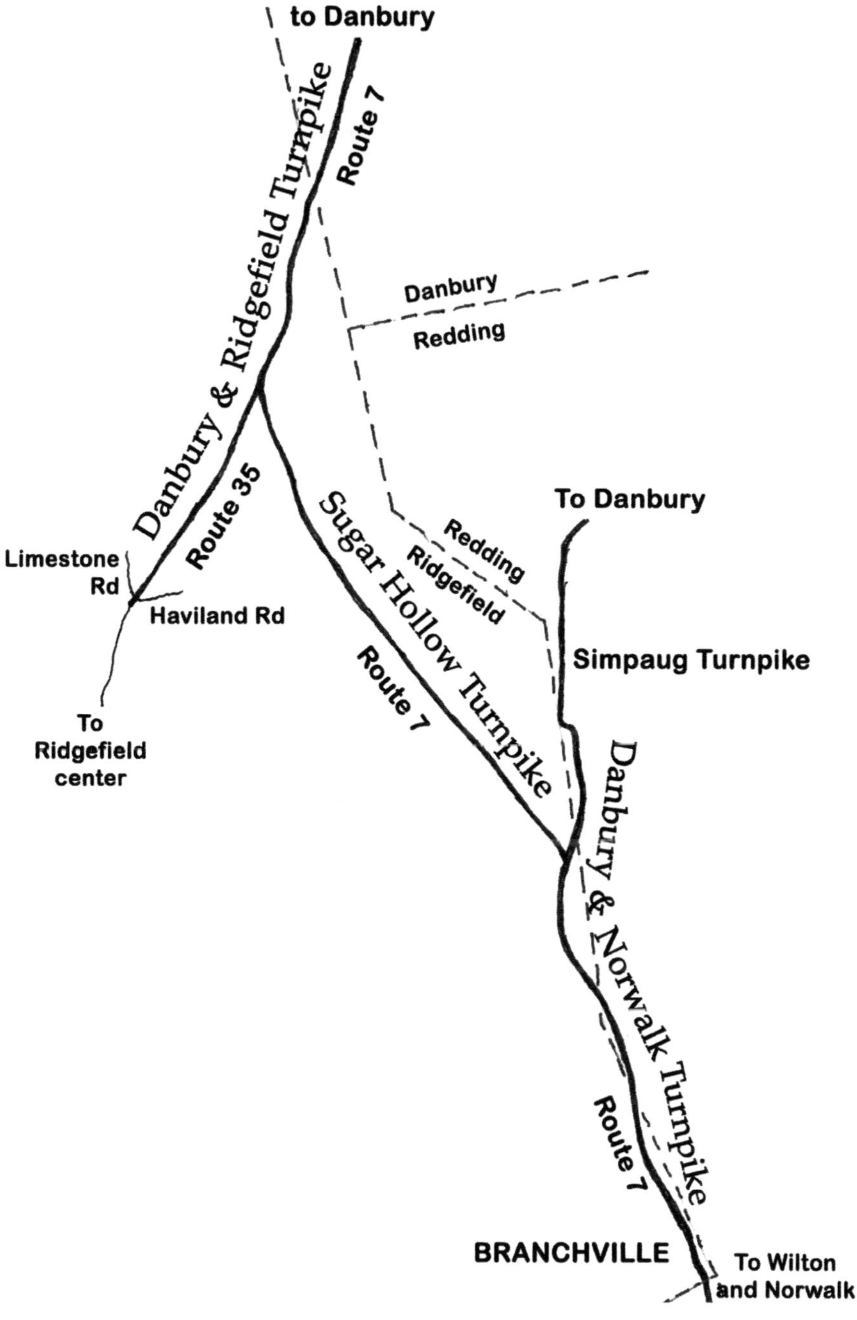

By 1840 or so, three turnpikes were operating in town, with the Sugar Hollow Turnpike connecting the northern and southern pikes. At some point, the Sugar Hollow and Danbury & Norwalk Turnpikes might have merged. *Map by author.*

and cities. So the state turned to a system already used in England: turnpikes, whose tolls would pay for road construction and maintenance.

Though there were some government-sponsored toll roads, private companies built and/or operated most of Connecticut's turnpikes. Along with Virginia, Connecticut was a pioneering state in toll road construction. Between 1795 and 1853, it granted 121 franchises to build and operate turnpikes.

One of the earliest toll roads in Connecticut ran though the southeastern corner of Ridgefield and was built by the Danbury and Norwalk Turnpike Company, incorporated in 1795. The southern end was in central Norwalk, at the Post Road. The northern end was in today's Bethel, which, back in 1795, was a parish of Danbury. The turnpike generally followed the path of today's Route 7 from Norwalk through Wilton Parish to Georgetown and then passed through today's Branchville section of Ridgefield on what is now called West Branchville Road. It then continued north via today's Route 7 to Simpaug Turnpike, which carried it through Redding to Route 53 and on the Bethel section of Danbury. The pike was eighteen miles long and apparently had only one tollgate.

Indications are that by the early 1800s, the company was in financial trouble and was not properly maintaining the road. There is also evidence that the route of the turnpike in Ridgefield eventually became part of the Sugar Hollow Turnpike.

The Danbury and Norwalk Turnpike probably made use of many already existing roads that were handed over to the company to maintain. However, some stretches, such as the one north of Branchville, had to be built from scratch.

The Danbury and Ridgefield Turnpike, incorporated in 1801, was almost an entirely new route. This road extended from the present intersection of Haviland and Limestone Roads north along the path of the present Danbury Road (Route 35) to Route 7 and then north over Route 7 through Sugar Hollow, coming out at the end of the runway at the south side of Danbury Airport.

Research by Ed Liljegren placed the site of a tollhouse for this turnpike just north of the Danbury line, on the west side of Route 7, a bit south of Bennett's Farm Road. The stone foundation, looking like a stone wall, stood very close to the road but was destroyed in the widening of Route 7 in 2005.

The Danbury and Ridgefield Turnpike Company was established by an act of the Connecticut General Assembly in May 1801, and by 1803, references to a "turnpike road" in this vicinity were appearing in the land records. Ridgefielders had been considering a new route to Danbury as early as 1787. The old "post road" to Danbury (see page 95) was rough, long and hilly, and the state government was pressing towns to improve inter-town highways. However, it appears that Danburians Joseph M. and Ebenezer B. White eventually got the ball rolling and built this road, for they were incorporated by the General Assembly as the "Danbury and Ridgefield Turnpike Company."

The Sugar Hollow Turnpike, incorporated in 1829, was the town's third and last toll road. Especially for western Danbury, it helped fulfill a need for a good route—and thus also good communication—between Danbury and Long Island Sound, with its shipping and, later, its shoreline railroad.

Although it bore the hollow's name, the turnpike did not actually run through Sugar Hollow, the gap between Wooster Mountain and Moses Mountain in Danbury. Instead, it met the Danbury and Ridgefield Turnpike, which had already accomplished that task.

The south end of the new Sugar Hollow Turnpike connected to the Danbury and Norwalk Turnpike at today's intersection of Route 7 and Simpaug Turnpike. It ran north almost in a straight line to meet the Danbury and Ridgefield Turnpike at today's intersection of Routes 7 and 35. Once up in Danbury via the Danbury and Ridgefield Turnpike, the northbound traveler could head off toward Danbury's village or could ride on the northern leg of the Sugar Hollow Turnpike, which began around the south end of today's Danbury Airport, headed over to Mill Plain via Kenosia Avenue and then continued northwesterly over Joe's Hill Road to the New York State line. At that time, today's Mill Plain and western Danbury were part of Ridgefield. Thus, this road provided a flatter route to connect the northern reaches of Ridgefield with the more developed southern section, using a road superior to the older, more direct combination of North Salem and Ridgebury Roads.

Today, it is almost impossible to figure out some of the old turnpike routes and owners because so few records exist, and deeds on the land records rarely deal with turnpikes. For instance, it's possible that the Sugar Hollow Turnpike owners eventually took over a portion of the old Danbury and Norwalk Turnpike between northern Wilton and Simpaug Turnpike, for their incorporation papers seem to give them the right to have a road from Wilton north through Ridgefield and on toward Danbury.

While ownership and routes may be unclear, the tolls charged for travel on the turnpikes are known because they were set by the General Assembly. In 1829, a resolution established the following rates:

On each four wheel pleasure carriage drawn by two horses, & on each stage 25 cents
On each two wheel pleasure carriage, drawn by one horse 12.5 cents
On each additional horse in a pleasure carriage, and on each person and horse 4 cents
On each sled, sleigh, car or wagon, drawn by one horse, ox or mule, or one yoke of oxen 6.3 cents
On each additional horse, ox or mule 2.5 cents
On horses, cattle, mules, each 1 cent
On sheep and swine, each 5 mills

Those tolls may seem low, but when you consider the relative value of money then, traveling a short distance by pleasure vehicle on a turnpike could be very expensive. Twenty-five cents in 1825 was worth about five dollars today.

There were exceptions to the tolls. "Persons travelling to and from public worship, funerals, society, town, or elector's meetings; all officers and soldiers going to or returning from military duty by order of law; all persons travelling to or from grist-mills, or in their ordinary farming business, shall not be liable to pay toll at said gate or gates, but shall be exempted therefrom," the state said.

Just when our three turnpikes stopped charging tolls is unclear, but in his book *The Turnpikes of New England*, Frederic J. Wood reports, "The Danbury and Ridgefield's charter was repealed in 1860 and, since the two roads were so interwoven, it seems probable that the Sugar Hollow became free at the same time, although no act to that effect has been found." (Wood was so confused by imprecise franchise descriptions that he misinterpreted the path of the road, incorrectly believing that the Sugar Hollow Turnpike came through Ridgefield's center via today's Routes 33 and 35.)

Turnpikes were not a successful business enterprise; Mr. Wood believed that hardly any of the more than one hundred turnpikes franchised in Connecticut ever made a profit. The arrival of the Danbury and Norwalk Rail Road eliminated any possible profitability for all three pikes in Ridgefield. Built in 1852, the railroad followed much of the same route as the old Danbury and Norwalk Turnpike and was able to transport freight and passengers much more quickly, comfortably and probably cheaply than the toll road. Freight wagons had been among the most regular and most lucrative customers of turnpikes, and the loss of their business doomed the toll roads.

Railroads also doomed another kind of toll highway before it even got started: the plank road. Plank roads, which had been built in other parts of the country, were highways paved with wooden planks, offering a smooth surface and eliminating the perennial problem of mud. However, the roads were expensive to build and maintain as planks wore out quickly. Of several plank roads authorized in Connecticut, only one was ever completed. Among those never built was that of the Stamford, New Canaan and Ridgefield Plank Road Company, franchised in 1851, that was intended to connect Ridgefield with Stamford.

THE AGE OF THE STAGE

Mass transit in Ridgefield began in the eighteenth century in the form of stagecoaches, but exactly when service started is not known. Historian Silvio Bedini seemed pretty certain that a New York–Boston stage line was running through town by the mid-1700s and that the Keeler Tavern on Main Street was serving as a stage stop by the 1770s.

On major routes, stagecoaches usually carried not only people but also mail. When Route 35, South Salem Road, enters New York State, it becomes the "Old Post Road" in Lewisboro. Clearly, if it was an "old post road" in Lewisboro, it was also an old one in Ridgefield, too, though that name never caught on here.

A post road was a long-distance mail route so called because it had "post houses," or post offices, along it. The word "post" referred to the stations, or "posts," that were set up in England along old mail routes where horses and mail could be exchanged. In the eighteenth and early nineteenth centuries, a post road was considered a major highway—the eighteenth-century equivalent of an interstate—because it passed through the centers of villages, was known to have food and lodging along it and was in decent condition, or decent for those days, at least.

Keep in mind that, before the late nineteenth century, roads were like today's wires or radio waves. Post roads carried not only people and mail but also news. Long before telephones, radios or the Internet, post roads were providing the latest bulletins of information in the form of newspapers, letters or simply verbal reports from passengers on board stages or on horseback.

For almost its whole length, today's Route 35 in Ridgefield was part of a "northern" post road from New York to Hartford and Boston, as opposed to

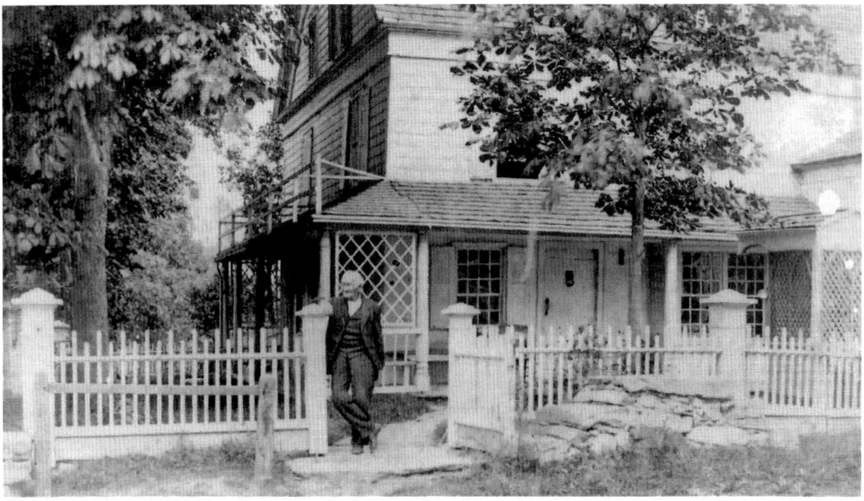

Innkeeper Abijah Resseguie is shown here in the 1880s at the Keeler Tavern, which he had operated for many years. The diary of his daughter, Anna Marie, is quoted in several places in this book. *Photograph courtesy of the Ridgefield Historical Society.*

the more famous "southern" one that is today called "the Boston Post Road," or U.S. Route 1. While none of the route in Ridgefield was ever formally called "Post Road," there were informal references to it. For instance, an 1843 property description mentions "the Post Road" when referring to what's now Main Street.

In the 1700s, a northbound stage on the post road route in Ridgefield would have entered town at the state line on Old South Salem Road and continued over South Salem Road, West Lane, Main Street, Danbury Road, Haviland Road and Picketts Ridge to beyond Great Pond into Redding. From there, the post road turned directly north, going through Starrs Plain and over Moses Mountain into Danbury. A little dead-end road off Wooster Heights in southern Danbury is today called "Old Boston Post Road," though people in the neighborhood might wonder why.

In the early 1800s, the Danbury and Ridgefield Turnpike was built in Sugar Hollow, making the post road route between the two towns much flatter (see page 91 for map).

In colonial times, Keeler Tavern was probably the town's post office and a stop for most or all stagecoaches. Situated in what was then the center of the Ridgefield business community, the tavern provided stage riders with an opportunity for refreshment while mail was being exchanged and perhaps horses changed.

By 1800, there was a Danbury and New York Stage. Historian Allan Nevins said that the southbound stage passed through Ridgefield every Monday, Wednesday and Friday while the northbound runs were Tuesday, Thursday and Saturday. "The fare from Danbury to Ridgefield was 55 cents, or about as much as a laborer could earn by a day's work; that from Ridgefield to New York was $2.90."

Nevins said the stage usually left New York with six horses and would drop two of them at White Plains, "where the passengers had thinned out, and unless there was an unusual load…leave two more at Northcastle." If the stage departed New York at 4:00 a.m., it could reach the Keeler Tavern by a little before 6:00 p.m., he said.

Riding in a stagecoach was often an unpleasant experience. In 1785, Josiah Quincy described a trip from Boston to New York:

> *The journey took up to a week, which in that day was considered a record of wonderful expedition. The carriages were old and worn. The harness was made of ropes. One pair of horses carried the stage 18 miles. We generally reached our resting place for the night, if no accident intervened, at 10 o'clock; and, after a frugal supper went to bed with a notice that we should be called at 3 the next morning, which generally proved to be half past two. Then, whether it snowed or rained, the traveler must rise and make ready by the help of a horn-lantern and a farthing candle, and proceed on his way over bad roads, sometimes with a driver showing no doubtful symptoms of drunkenness, which good-hearted passengers never failed to improve at every stopping place by urging upon him another glass of toddy.*

If the stage got stuck in mud, the passengers got out—often in the rain—and helped push it out.

Stagecoach drivers often came from the ranks of the men who started out as mail riders, men who carried mail sacks on a horse like the famous Pony Express. They knew horses and roads and were well "weather-beaten" already. Such was the case with David Hunt, who started Ridgefield's first stage line in 1836. Hunt, who had been a mail rider from Ridgefield to Stamford and to Peekskill, saw a need for passenger service to the steamboat dock in South Norwalk, where one could travel in a comfortable vessel to New York City instead of being battered and bounced in a stage on forty miles of poor roads.

Hunt lived on Old Stagecoach Road, just below Ridgebury Road. Here, the four-horse stage left at two thirty in the morning bound for Norwalk

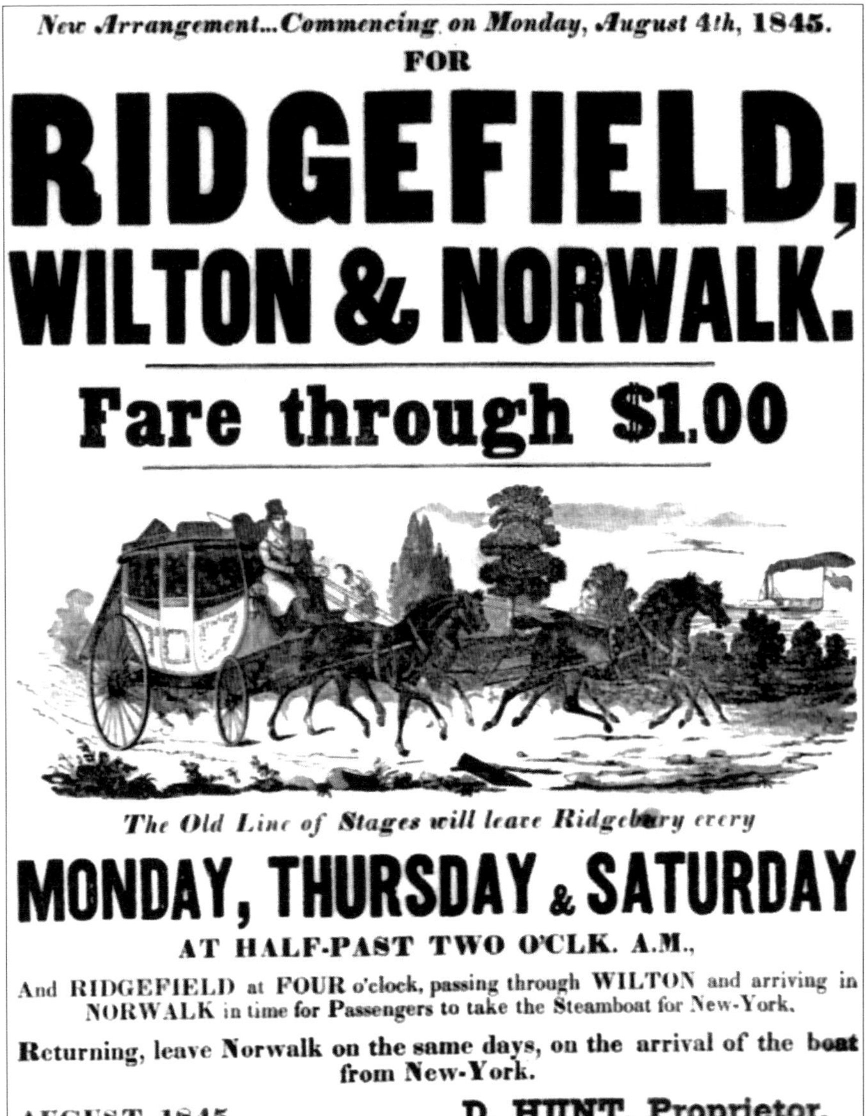

This 1845 poster advertised the stage service from Ridgebury to Norwalk, begun nine years earlier by former mail rider David Hunt. *From the* Ridgefield Press *archives*.

to meet the New York–bound steamboat. It made stops at such places as Titicus and Wilton Center. In Norwalk, the stage picked up a fresh set of horses while it waited for the next boat arriving from New York. Passengers traveling this stage line could get rides from Danbury, Mill

Plain and other areas to the north to the Hunt house, where they awaited the stage's early morning departure.

Bedini reports that Henry Whitney Hunt operated the Ridgefield to Stamford Stage Line for a while from his home in Scotland District to Stamford. Hunt lived in a farmhouse later owned by Francis D. Martin on the North Salem Road, just north of Ridgefield High School.

All this was in the days before the railroad. When the New York and New Haven's coastal line was opened in 1847 and the Danbury to Norwalk line followed in 1852, David Hunt's run to Norwalk and even Henry Hunt's to Stamford were made old-fashioned and tedious. However, Henry Whitlock operated a Ridgefield-to-Branchville stage for passengers and mail from 1852 until 1870, when the Branchville-to-Ridgefield train branch was built and eliminated its need. "Whitlock had earlier achieved some note," Bedini said. "As a boy of twelve he had driven a stage from Danbury to Norwalk and back again with four horses."

Today, a reminder of the old stage services is found in the name, Old Stagecoach Road, recalling the first part of Hunt's route from his house over Ridgebury Mountain and down to the Titicus Valley toward town and the Sound.

THE SHOW MUST GO ON

A stage of a different sort provided entertainment, not transportation. And while Ridgefield has been home to many "theater people," it took decades for live theater to really catch on in the community.

The earliest staged productions usually featured traveling artists, often just one actor. For instance, in August 1877, a twenty-four-year-old named William H. Gillette gave a performance in town hall. Gillette went on to become a world-famous actor, known especially for his portrayal of Sherlock Holmes. (In 1919, after five years of construction, his sizable stone mansion on the Connecticut River in Hadlyme was completed. Today, it is the central attraction of Gillette Castle State Park.)

In January 1882, two farces, *Rough Diamond* and *Lad from the Country*, were staged at the town hall. The "W.M.C. Band" provided music. Tickets were twenty-five cents. Even attorneys got into the act, as it were. In November 1886, a lawyer named Mr. Hodges staged a "defense of Richard III" on the town hall stage.

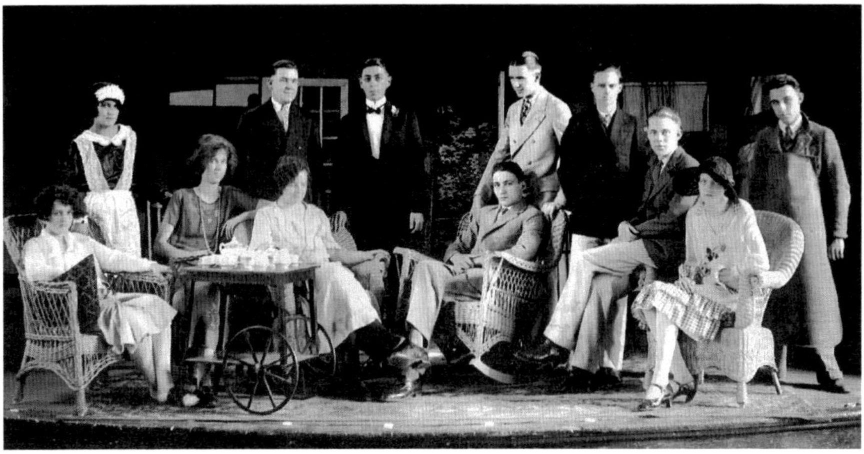

The cast of *Polly with a Past*, the 1926 Ridgefield High School senior play. *From left*: Alice Benjamin (Camp), Anne Casagrande (Girolmetti), Catherine Tobin, George Camp, Josephine Browse, Levio Zandri, John Bacchiochi, Albert Keeler, Harvey Keeler, Karl Nash, Ruth Johnson (Anderson) and Belden Nicholas. *Joseph Hartmann photograph, from the* Ridgefield Press *archives.*

In the 1920s and '30s, live theater in Ridgefield often took the form of the Ridgefield High School senior class plays. Each year, an elaborate production was staged in town hall, featuring nearly the entire senior class. Productions included *Daddy Long Legs* (1925), *Hiawatha* (1931), *Washington's Operetta* (1932), *China Boy* (1941) and *Patton's Muscle B Ranch* (1947). In 1927, even the faculty staged a play at the town hall, *The Adventures of Grandpa*. Bet *that* was a knee-slapper!

Church groups also put on plays. For instance, the Epworth League, a group for Methodist young adults, staged the three-act mystery comedy *Oh Kay* in town hall in January 1930.

By the late 1930s, the town began to attract summer theaters, but they struggled to be successful. "One of the favorite topics of speculation among stage folk and stage-struck folk is what makes a summer theater go in one town and fall in another," the *Ridgefield Press* mused in 1950 as it examined the failure of several attempts at summer theaters in town.

The failures certainly weren't due to a lack of talent. The first summer theater season here was in 1938, when producers Tano Sylvestro and Flora MacDonald opened in the First Congregational Church House with a comedy about Scandinavian marriage customs, *The Latitude of Love*. It starred two at the time little-known youngsters, Uta Hagen and José Ferrer. Hagen went on to earn three Tony Awards and originated the role of Martha in

Edward Albee's *Who's Afraid of Virginia Woolf*. Ferrer, who was Puerto Rican, became the first Hispanic actor to win an Academy Award, for his portrayal of Cyrano de Bergerac in the 1950 film; he also won a Tony for the stage version. Oh, yes, while doing the Ridgefield show, Hagen and Ferrer fell in love and were married that December. They often performed together, among the few husband-and-wife acting teams to become stars together. The marriage lasted ten years, perhaps long by Hollywood standards.

Despite having actors of that quality, the venture did not prosper. After six weeks, the theater was offering two-for-the-price-of-one tickets, and a *Ridgefield Press* editorial was urging the town to get out and support the shows. Nonetheless, a few weeks later, when Walter Hampden—a noted Shakespearian stage and movie actor who lived in town—appeared in a production at the theater, attendance was again sparse. Reviewing that play, *Press* publisher and editor Karl S. Nash wondered "whether or not the town of Ridgefield ought to be blown off the map for failing adequately to express its enthusiasm for its distinguished actor-citizen, Walter Hampden."

Sylvestro and McDonald did not return for another season, but the next year, Ridgefielder Philip Carr joined Alfred Wagstaff III in forming a new producing team that opened as the New England Playhouse at the Congregational Church House. In an editorial entitled "Straw-hat," the *Press* hoped better management would result in better attendance. The resident company included Philip Bourneuf (a stage, screen and TV actor), Frances Reid (who played Alice Horton in the TV soaper *Days of Our Lives* for forty-three years), Winston O'Keefe (later producer of the long-running *Dennis the Menace* TV series), Helen Shields (who later was on the soap opera *As the World Turns*) and Everett Ripley (who performed in many Shakespearian plays on Broadway). They drew enthusiastic notices from reviewers throughout the summer. But again, the audiences were poor—until, that is, a pre-Broadway tryout of *Gentlemen Prefer Blondes*, starring Marie Wilson, came to town; it filled the theater every night. But a packed house of 250 couldn't support the costs of a lavish show, complete with movie stars. Nevertheless, Carr was encouraged by the *Blondes* success and returned for the next season.

In an effort to gain publicity, the 1940 season began with a private show for the press, at which Walter Hampden read scenes from *Hamlet* and *Cyrano* and singer-actress Jane Pickens performed songs. Among the shows that summer was *The Night of January 16th*, starring actress Gloria Stuart as a woman on trial for murder. Each night, a group of prominent local people was chosen to sit in the jury box and, at the end of the drama, decide whether Stuart were guilty or innocent (she was judged guilty three times and not guilty,

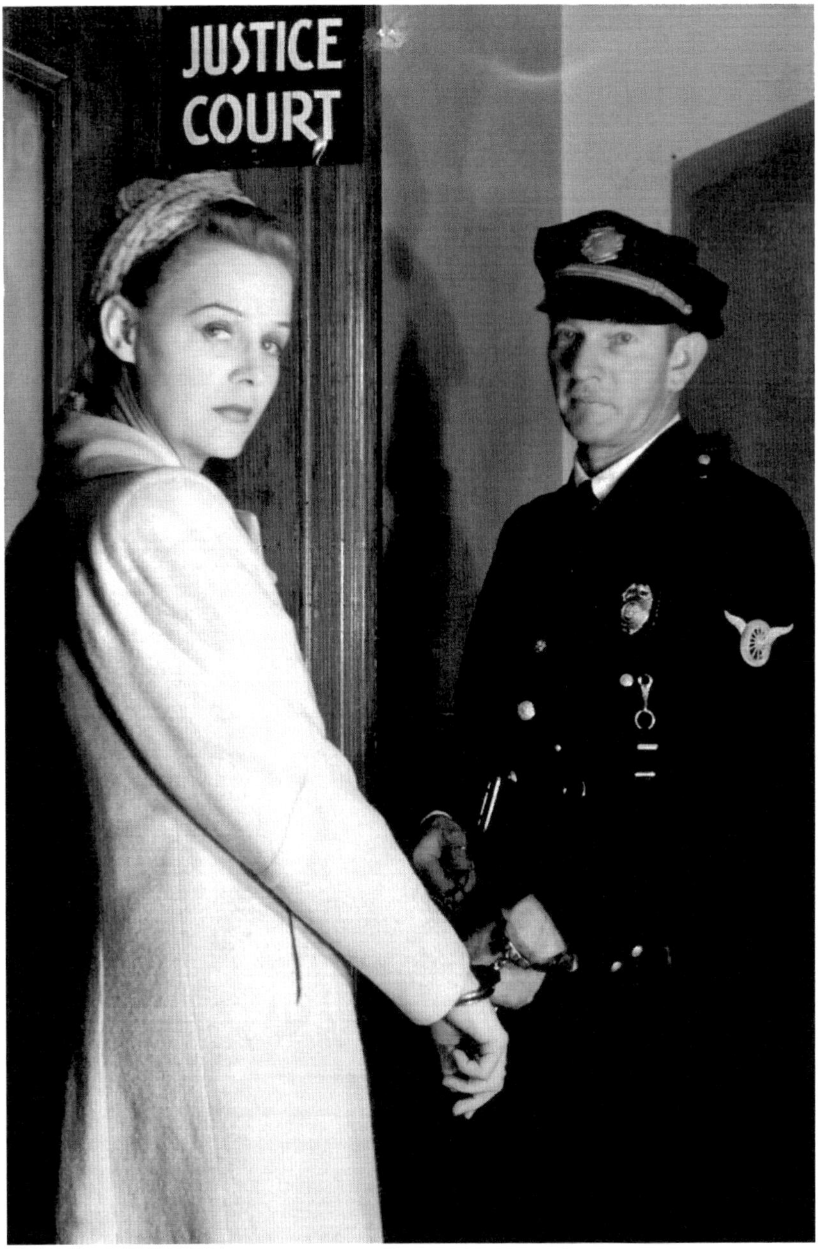

Ridgefield constable Gux Rux posed in town hall with actress Gloria Stuart for a 1940 Ridgefield Summer Theater production in which Rux had a small part. Fifty-seven years later, Stuart was nominated for an Academy Award for portraying a one-hundred-year-old woman in *Titanic*; she was eighty-seven. *Robert R. Keeler, photograph, from* Ridgefield Press *archives.*

four). This is the same Gloria Stuart who, at the age of eighty-seven, played the one-hundred-year-old Rose in the film *Titanic*. She was nominated in 1997 for an Academy Award for Best Supporting Actress—the oldest person ever nominated for an Oscar for acting.

Even the audience-participation shows did not draw crowded houses, and the *Press* soon warned, "Unless there is a substantial increase in attendance next week, the New England Playhouse will be forced to give up the ghost." But when Paul and Grace Hartman, a famous vaudeville dancing and comedy team, appeared, the audiences filled the house; attendees included Gene Tunney, the world heavyweight boxing champion, and Brenda Frazier, a wealthy socialite whom the media had dubbed "the poor little rich girl." The show was held over four extra days and closed the season on a hopeful note. However, worries over war apparently dashed any plans for the 1941 season.

Seven years later, the press carried a headline, "Broadway Actors Organize New Summer Theatre." The group included Allyn Rice, a radio actress; Carl Jacobs, "recently of the Old Vic"; and Alexander Kirkland, an actor and director. They promised the top ticket price would be $1.98. The company leased the Ridgefield High School auditorium (now the Ridgefield Playhouse), which was twice as big as the old Congregational Church House, opening a nine-week season in late June with *Rip Van Winkle*. The subject may have presaged the sleepy season. Attendance was poor, and the effort ended with what was reported to have been a heavy financial loss.

However, Jacobs and Kirkland were encouraged by the fact that attendance picked up at the end of the season and returned the next year, offering such shows as *Springtime for Henry*, an Edward Everett Horton farce, and *All the Way Home*, a pre-Broadway play by Lynn Riggs, author of *Green Grow the Lilacs*. Audiences remained lackluster despite efforts to stimulate attendance, such as $2.94 tickets and $0.50 matinees for teenagers. "At the close of the second season, the producers announced that there would be no third season unless the townspeople showed more interest in the theater," the *Press* reported. There was no third season.

By the 1950s, the fortunes of live theater in Ridgefield were changing. Not only was the town growing in population—and potential audiences—but local thespians were also taking a different tack, offering year-round amateur productions instead of summer-only professional shows. A leader in the amateur theater movement was Joseph M. Dunworth, who started the Ridgefield Players, an amateur theater group that staged shows for a while in the 1950s. Then Dunworth, Evelyn Foley and Patricia DiMuzio decided in

1965 to form the Ridgefield Workshop for the Performing Arts (RWPA) for not only staging shows but also "fostering and developing creative talent." Its first production, one-act performances of *Sorry, Wrong Number* and the second act from *Auntie Mame*, took place that November.

One of the problems that led to the demise of the Ridgefield Players in the 1950s was a lack of a suitable space, but thanks to the town government, the RWPA was able to use several buildings, finally settling into a small old barn on the former Holy Ghost Novitiate property on Prospect Ridge. The town had purchased the novitiate, its outbuildings and land in 1971, and the property is now largely used for congregate and affordable housing, as well as playing fields, an artists' studio/gallery and a dog playground called the Bark Park. Over the years, the theater group has rebuilt and modernized the barn to make it a comfortable venue.

The workshop went on to stage scores of productions, including musicals, mysteries, comedies and children's shows. Eventually, the RWPA became today's Ridgefield Theater Barn, a thriving operation that has been so successful that it sells out most of its many shows and, in 2015—its fiftieth-anniversary year—was planning a $750,000 building addition that includes a new black-box theater area for smaller, more intimate programs; space for a two-person office and a costume room; and ground-level rooms for classes and conferences. "We've grown quite tremendously," Wayne Leiss, the theater's executive director, told the *Press*. "We're doing 33 weekend performances a year and what we've found out is that's a really high use for the space we have."

Despite years of trials and tribulations with pros on the stage, live theater is thriving in Ridgefield today with amateurs doing the shows.

THE ALMIGHTY ALMANAC

A different kind of entertainment was provided closer to home in the nineteenth century. Its existence was briefly noted by Jared Nash, a farmer who lived on Silver Spring Road opposite St. Johns Road, when he recorded in his diary on Friday, December 29, 1865: "Clear and pleasant. Cut some wood. Father & Mother went to Mr. Holmes in afternoon, & father went to post office and Bailey's and got a new Almanack for 1866."

For most nineteenth-century farmers here, the two most important printed documents in their homes were the Bible and the current almanac. The

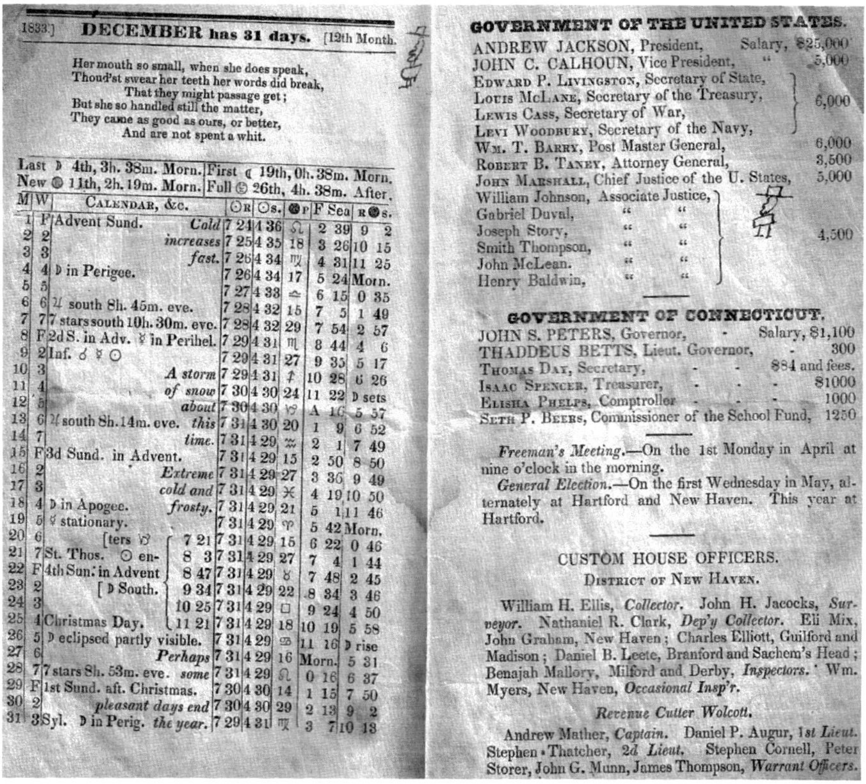

1833.] **DECEMBER has 31 days.** [12th Month.

Her mouth so small, when she does speak,
Thoud'st swear her teeth her words did break,
That they might passage get;
But she so handled still the matter,
They came as good as ours, or better,
And are not spent a whit.

Last ☽ 4th, 3h. 38m. Morn.	First ☾ 19th, 0h. 38m. Morn.
New ● 11th, 2h. 19m. Morn.	Full ○ 26th, 4h. 38m. After.

M	W	CALENDAR, &c.	☉ R	☉ S.	☽ P	F Sea	R ☽ S.
1	F	Advent Sund. *Cold*	7 24	4 36	♌	2 39	9 2
2	2	*increases*	7 25	4 35	18	3 26	10 15
3	3	*fast.*	7 26	4 34	♍	4 31	11 25
4	4	☽ in Perigee.	7 26	4 34	17	5 24	Morn.
5	5		7 27	4 33	♎	6 15	0 35
6	6	♃ south 8h. 45m. eve.	7 28	4 32	15	7 5	1 49
7	7	7 stars south 10h. 30m. eve.	7 28	4 32	29	7 54	2 57
8	F	2d S. in Adv. ☿ in Perihel.	7 29	4 31	♏	8 44	4 6
9	2	Inf. ☌ ☿ ☉	7 29	4 31	27	9 35	5 17
10	3	*A storm*	7 29	4 31	♐	10 28	6 26
11	4	*of snow*	7 30	4 30	24	11 22	☽ sets
12	5	*about*	7 30	4 30	♑	A 16	5 57
13	6	♃ south 8h. 14m. eve. *this*	7 31	4 30	20	1 9	6 52
14	7	*time.*	7 31	4 29	♒	2 1	7 49
15	F	3d Sund. in Advent.	7 31	4 29	15	2 50	8 50
16	2	*Extreme*	7 31	4 29	27	3 36	9 49
17	3	*cold and*	7 31	4 29	♓	4 19	10 50
18	4	☽ in Apogee. *frosty.*	7 31	4 29	21	5 1	11 46
19	5	☿ stationary.	7 31	4 29	♈	5 42	Morn.
20	6	[ters ♑ 7 21	7 31	4 29	15	6 22	0 46
21	7	St. Thos. ☉ en- 8 3	7 31	4 29	27	7 4	1 44
22	F	4th Sun. in Advent 8 47	7 31	4 29	♉	7 48	2 45
23	2	[☽ South. 9 34	7 31	4 29	22	8 34	3 46
24	3	10 25	7 31	4 29	□	9 24	4 50
25	4	Christmas Day. 11 21	7 31	4 29	18	10 19	5 58
26	5	☽ eclipsed partly visible.	7 31	4 29	♋	11 16	☽ rise
27	6	*Perhaps*	7 31	4 29	16	Morn.	5 31
28	7	7 stars 8h. 53m. eve. *some*	7 31	4 29	♌	0 16	6 37
29	F	1st Sund. aft. Christmas.	7 30	4 30	14	1 15	7 50
30	2	*pleasant days end*	7 30	4 30	29	2 13	9 2
31	3	Syl. ☽ in Perig. *the year.*	7 29	4 31	♍	3 7	10 13

GOVERNMENT OF THE UNITED STATES.

ANDREW JACKSON, President, Salary, $25,000
JOHN C. CALHOUN, Vice President, " 5,000
EDWARD P. LIVINGSTON, Secretary of State,
LOUIS McLANE, Secretary of the Treasury,
LEWIS CASS, Secretary of War,
LEVI WOODBURY, Secretary of the Navy, } 6,000
WM. T. BARRY, Post Master General, 6,000
ROBERT B. TANEY, Attorney General, 3,500
JOHN MARSHALL, Chief Justice of the U. States, 5,000
William Johnson, Associate Justice,
Gabriel Duval, " "
Joseph Story, " "
Smith Thompson, " "
John McLean. " "
Henry Baldwin, " " } 4,500

GOVERNMENT OF CONNECTICUT.

JOHN S. PETERS, Governor, - Salary, $1,100
THADDEUS BETTS, Lieut. Governor, - 300
THOMAS DAY, Secretary, - - $84 and fees.
ISAAC SPENCER, Treasurer, - - - $1000
ELISHA PHELPS, Comptroller - - - 1000
SETH P. BEERS, Commissioner of the School Fund, 1250

Freeman's Meeting.—On the 1st Monday in April at nine o'clock in the morning.

General Election.—On the first Wednesday in May, alternately at Hartford and New Haven. This year at Hartford.

CUSTOM HOUSE OFFICERS.

DISTRICT OF NEW HAVEN.

William H. Ellis, *Collector.* John H. Jacocks, *Surveyor.* Nathaniel R. Clark, *Dep'y Collector.* Eli Mix, John Graham, New Haven; Charles Elliott, Guilford and Madison; Daniel B. Leete, Branford and Sachem's Head; Benajah Mallory, Milford and Derby, *Inspectors.* Wm. Myers, New Haven, *Occasional Insp'r.*

Revenue Cutter Wolcott.

Andrew Mather, *Captain.* Daniel P. Augur, *1st Lieut.* Stephen Thatcher, *2d Lieut.* Stephen Cornell, Peter Storer, John G. Munn, James Thompson, *Warrant Officers.*

Two pages from *Prindle's Almanac* for 1833, published in New Haven. The doodles on both pages were probably the work of a child of the era. *Author's collection.*

former gave spiritual advice while the latter helped with the more mundane aspects of everyday life.

The almanac told the basics, such as the risings and settings of the sun and moon and the phases of the latter—information that was important when a farmer was planning plantings or a harvest and needed to work at night under a full moon. Almanacs often predicted local weather, though their abilities at prognostication were, of course, questionable.

More important to farmers, agricultural almanacs, such as the still-published *Old Farmers Almanac*, advised on the best times to plant, reported new farming techniques and offered tips for homemakers. Many contained recipes, humorous anecdotes and bits of history. They served as a combination of news, education and entertainment.

The earliest American almanac was published in Cambridge, Massachusetts, in 1639. Over the next two centuries, a variety of almanacs

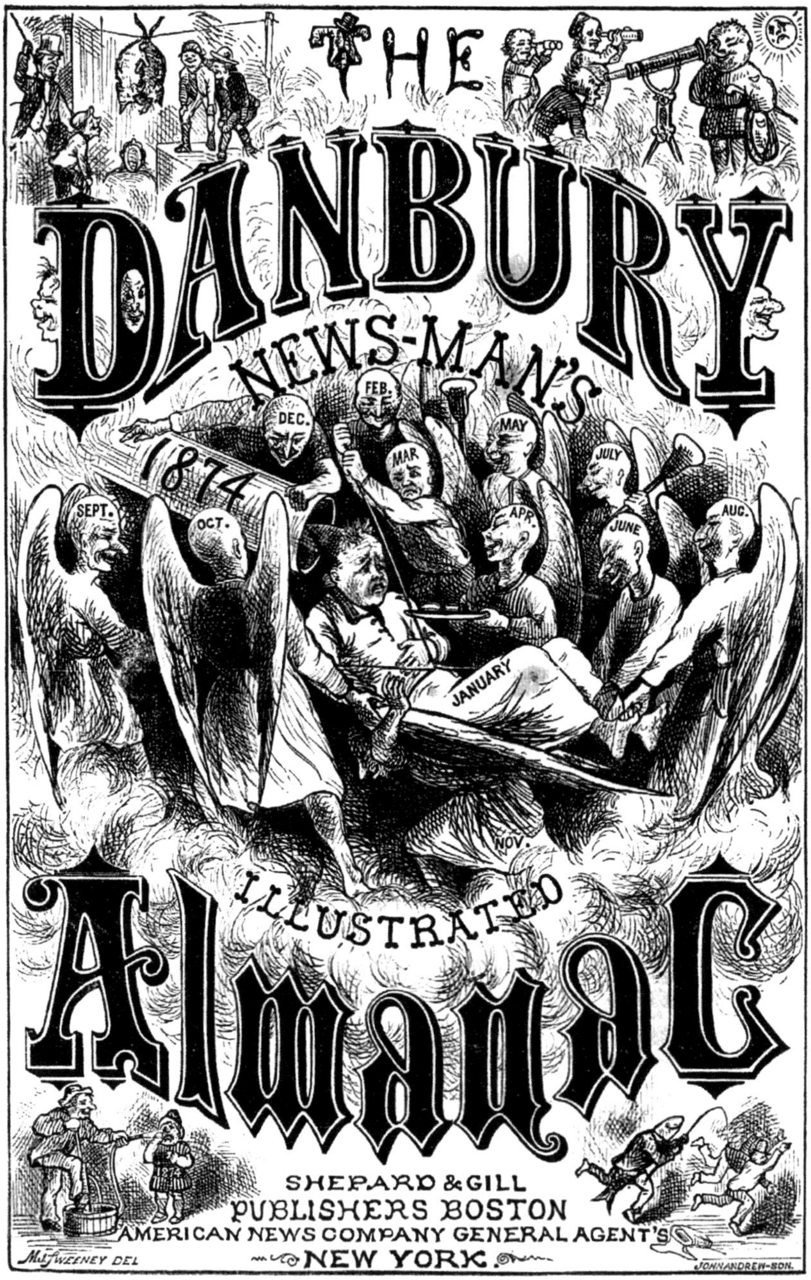

Beers' atlas of Fairfield County shows a "lecture room" and "sheds" on the north side of Branchville Road (R.R. Avenue). The Sabbath Day house was probably there. *Author's collection.*

came and went. By the 1860s, at least a dozen different ones were in circulation in the Northeast.

It's hard to tell what almanac Jared Nash's father purchased or what the average Ridgefield farmer used, but almanacs could be quite local. The *Old Farmers Almanac*, the most famous and widespread almanac, had localized editions in many major northeastern cities. *The New England Almanac and Farmer's Friend* was printed by a number of companies—author David Daboll produced the main body of data and text, selling it to local printers who, in turn, sold ads around it and put their own names and addresses on the cover. *Middlebrook's New England Almanac* had a Norwalk edition that was based on calculations for Bridgeport.

The most unusual almanac that Ridgefielders might acquire was *The Danbury News-Man's Illustrated Almanac*, produced by the lively and literate writer James M. Bailey (1841–1894). A Civil War veteran, Bailey published and edited the *Danbury News*, an ancestor of today's *News-Times*, and was known as "the Danbury News Man." He became so famous for his many humorous articles in the *News* that people across the country subscribed to the newspaper for its entertainment value. The same sense of humor filled the pages of his almanacs.

For instance, while recalling his childhood, he described the bright, new yellow-covered almanac in January that, twelve months later, had covers that "were rolled up, or gone, and there were conveniences for telling pretty accurately how many flies had enjoyed its retirement." Its calendar, he said, was where "the weather was handled, and where drunken-looking moons, and improbable suns, and highly impossible tides were made to go through performances that were intensely edifying to the family."

In an introduction to his 1874 almanac, Bailey wrote, "There are very few men who do not remember, or cannot recall, the importance the almanac enjoyed in his boyhood's home. I remember it used to hang by a string to the kitchen wall; and the member of the family who took it down for reference was required to hang it up again when through with it."

The almanacs were famous for their promotions of patent medicines as well as the recipes offered to the household cooks of the day. "Endorsements from well-known physicians in unknown localities" were often mixed in with "recipes for making puddings that no one should eat, and cake that no one would dare to," Bailey wrote. "And when a recipe for either was hedged in by the details of a fever-sore on one side, and the graphic particulars of a hemorrhage on the other, the symmetry of the whole was undeniable."

In 1874, Bailey published a book of his humorous almanac and newspaper writings, called *Life in Danbury by the Danbury News Man*. On his serious side, Bailey went on to compile the first history of Danbury but died before it could be completed. That job was taken up by Susan Benedict Hill, who organized his work and published it as the 583-page *History of Danbury* in 1896, two years after Bailey's death.

Many nineteenth-century almanacs were provided free of charge, but they were largely advertising vehicles. Various manufacturers offered almanacs to help sell their products. Among them was *A.L. Scovill & Company's Almanac*, which provided basic almanac data but whose text was largely devoted to describing illnesses and how they could be treated with such Scovill products as Dr. Wm. Hall's Balsam for the Lungs, Dr. Mott's Vegetable Liver Pills and Dr. Baker's Pain Panacea. Dr. J.C. Ayer and Company produced *Ayer's American Almanac*, offering descriptions of and testimonials for Ayer patent medicines. The Lodi Manufacturing Company in New York published *The Farmers and Planters Almanac*, which helped it peddle its fertilizer products.

Even religions had almanacs. For example, *The Methodist Almanac*, published in New York City, contained both practical and spiritual advice, as well as plenty of ads for organs, prayer books and life insurance.

TOASTING YOUR TOES IN A CHILLY CHURCH

Speaking of Methodists, attending church services in eighteenth-century Ridgefield could be a numbing experience, and not because of what the preacher said. In winter, church buildings were flat-out frigid. The Congregational Church on the Village Green, for instance, had no fireplace or stove in the 1700s, and temperatures could dip well below zero in January and February.

"Women and children were allowed in mid-winter to bring foot-stoves to the church to mitigate the cold during the hour-long sermon, for the wind whistled through a score of cracks," wrote Allan Nevins in his *An Historical Sketch of Ridgefield*. "But had any man…used them, they would have been indelibly disgraced."

In his 1975 history of St. Stephen's Church, Robert Haight said that early in the 1800s, sermons by the local rector could last up to an hour and a half. "On cold wintry days, when the churches had minimal heat or none, this could test the depth of one's Christian commitment." Indications are that

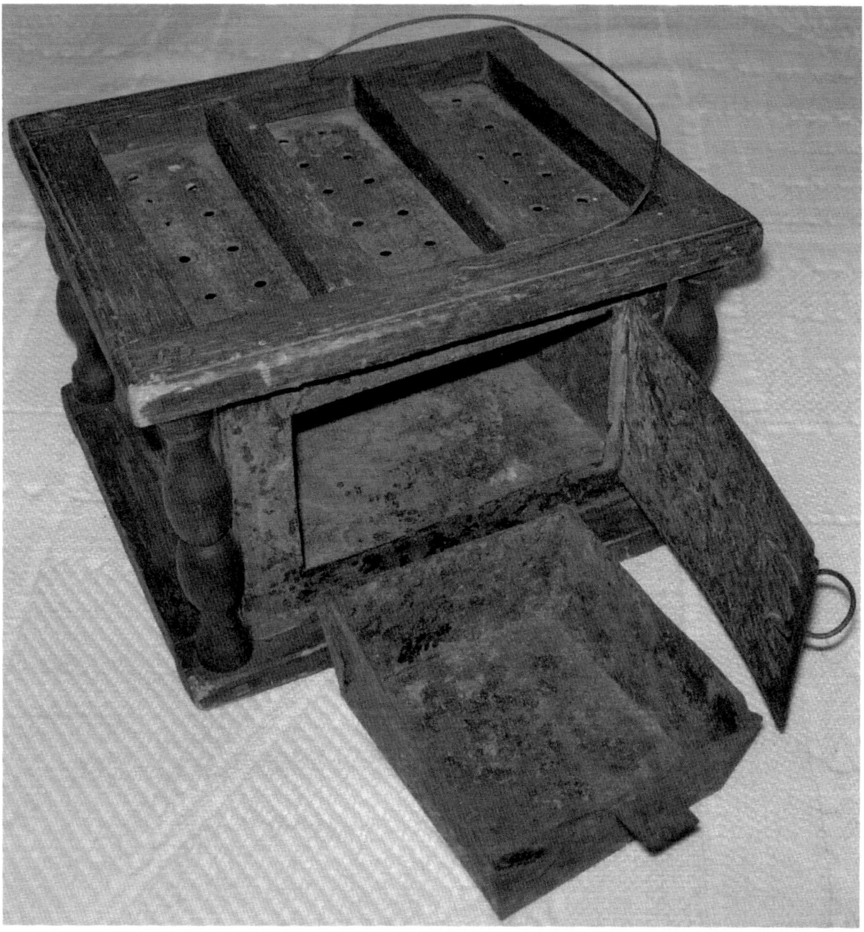

Women in the eighteenth century might use foot stoves like this one to keep warm in church. The tray held coals brought from home. Foot stoves were also used for keeping toasty in carriages and stages. *Courtesy of Larry D. Smith, motherbedford.com.*

the Episcopal church buildings used both before and after the Revolution had no heat at all.

How cold could it get? Anna Marie Resseguie recorded in her diary at the Keeler Tavern on February 7, 1855, "Very exceeding cold. *The Tribune* says such cold weather had not been known in N.Y. City in 20 years…At Mr. Short's this morning, about sunrise, the mercury was 17 degrees below zero. It froze in every room of our house where there was anything to freeze."

Heating a church building was difficult. It was a large open space, surrounded by walls that were not well sealed, much less insulated. Since

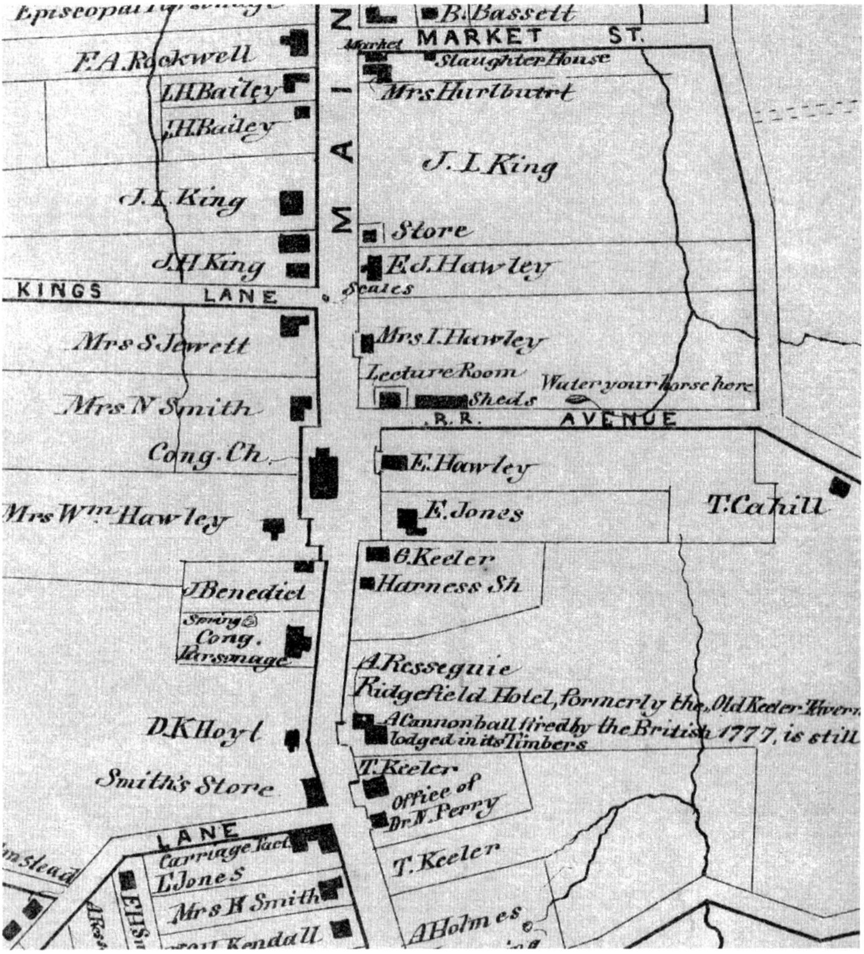

Clark's map of Fairfield County in 1856 shows a "session" house on the north side of Branchville Road, just before it meets Main Street. The Sabbath Day house was probably here. *University of Connecticut MAGIC historical map collection.*

the building was not in daily use, church leaders probably did not consider warmth a critical need, especially since frigid days were limited to the winter—when there could also be relatively mild periods.

However, Ridgefield Congregationalists had a special way of dealing with the cold. Minutes of the town meeting for April 17, 1749, indicate voters authorized the construction of a "Sabbath Day house" up to twelve by ten feet in size. Popular in New England, a Sabbath Day house was a small building with a fireplace where families could warm up and

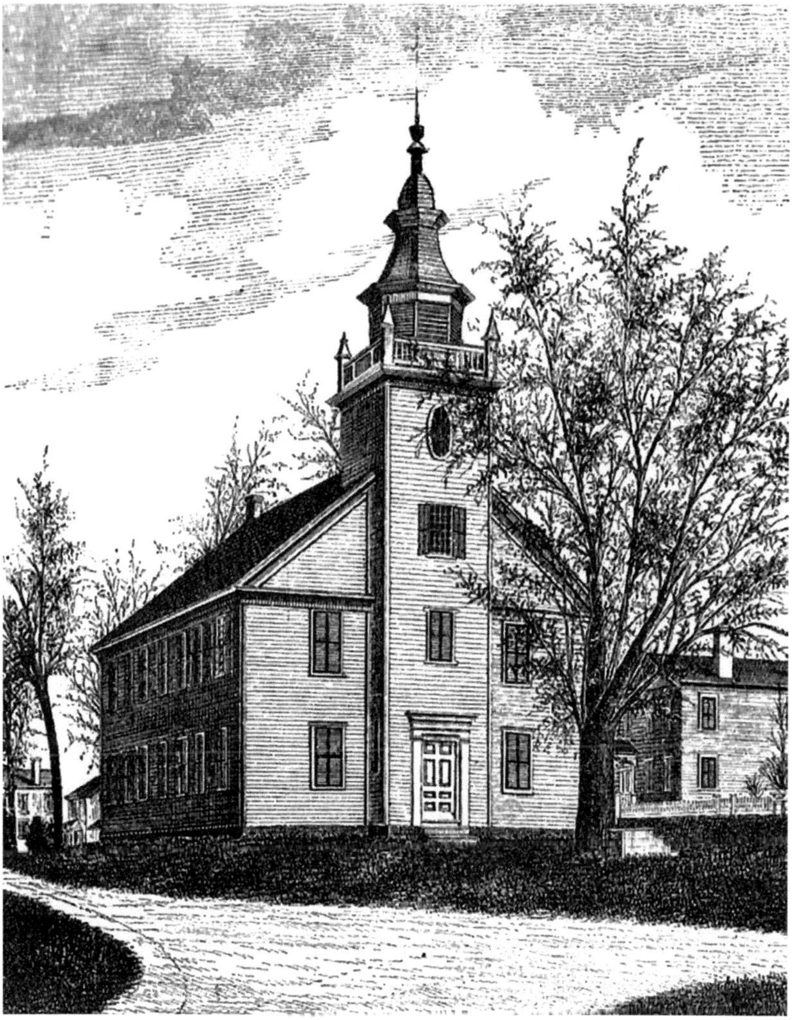

This edition of the Congregational meetinghouse, which stood on the village green from 1800 until around 1888, was no doubt the site of many icy services. But at least toward the end of its days, it had some form of heat—a small stove-type chimney is visible at its rear. *From* History of Ridgefield *by Reverend Daniel W. Teller.*

have a bite to eat during breaks in the long services on Sundays at the unheated church—or "meetinghouse," as it was called in the eighteenth century. This Sabbath Day house was just across Main Street from the Congregational Church building.

It was not until well into the nineteenth century that churches began installing heating systems, usually stoves. Old images from the 1870s and

'80s indicate that the Congregational Church on the Green by then had a small stove-sized chimney at its rear end. While stoves could not heat a church the way modern furnaces can, they could take the chill off a frigid Sunday service.

The Sabbath Day house probably had additional functions or acquired them as the congregation grew. It could be a place for church hierarchy meetings, lectures or small group lessons, such as Sunday school. Clark's 1856 map of Fairfield County shows a "Session H. Cong. Ch." on the north side of Branchville Road, a few dozen feet before Main Street and not far from the church on the Village Green. "Session House" was a term for a place where church leaders met; in the Presbyterian Church, a "session" was a body of governing elders. By 1867, when Beers' map of Ridgefield was published, the building was labeled a "lecture room." This structure might have been an expanded version of the old Sabbath Day house or an entirely new building on the same site.

The Sabbath Day/Session house was probably torn down or moved elsewhere when the new First Congregational Church opened in 1888 at the corner of Main Street and West Lane. This stone edifice was well sealed and heated.

OUR IRON AGE

On North Salem Road, near where the Garden of Ideas is today, Ridgefielders once had a business that was about as far from gardening as could be imagined: iron smelting. Deeds in the late 1700s and early 1800s mention the "Iron Works" in that neighborhood. While it was apparently a short-lived operation, the ironworks was one of the few seriously "industrial" operations, albeit on a small scale, in early Ridgefield.

Iron was the most important metal to the settlers. From it were made the tools that built houses and barns and the nails that held, along with the latches and hinges that operated doors, parts of them together. Farm implements were forged of iron, as were the shoes for horses and axles for carts and coaches. Kitchen utensils, including pots and peels, ladles, forks and knives, were all made of iron.

In 1789, Timothy Keeler Jr., Nathan Dauchy and Elijah Keeler built a pond to serve a new ironworks along the stream that flows out of Lake Mamanasco. The works were in operation a year later. However, by 1797, a deed refers to land situated "where the Iron Works lately stood." Even as late as 1834, deeds define locations as near or at "where the old Iron Works stood."

Where it stood was along North Salem Road between Sherwood and Ridgebury Roads, in the little valley through which the stream from Mamanasco flows to the Titicus River. Across the highway—south of Craigmoor Road—is what's left of the pond, long called Forge Pond because the ironworks used its waters. After the ironworks ceased functioning, the pond powered grist- and sawmills on or near the old works site. Today, the pond has become a natural wetland, part of the Garden of Ideas.

The ironworks probably converted iron ore to pig iron. Whether various implements were then manufactured from the iron at that location is unknown. Certainly local blacksmiths could have at least gotten their supply of iron there.

The usual ironworks included a twenty- to forty-foot-high stone furnace. Ore was heated to melting in crucibles inside the furnace, and the impure slag that rose to the top was skimmed off. The pond's water was needed to operate the huge bellows that would pump air onto the fire. Because it wasn't easy to build up the 2,200-degree heat needed for refining, many furnaces ran constantly and were shut down for only repairs or cleaning.

While there was no rail or water transportation to bring in large quantities of ore, iron was available in Ridgefield. A 1792 map of Connecticut, drawn by Samuel Huntington, bears the legend "iron mines" in a section of Ridgebury north of George Washington Highway and along Briar Ridge Road. This map is not known for its accuracy in placing landmarks, but it nonetheless makes clear that iron mines existed in northern Ridgefield at the time the ironworks was in operation. It is quite possible that the works got its ore from there.

Iron ore was also found not far from town. In the Brewster section of Southeast, New York, which borders Ridgefield on the northwest, iron mines were operating from the mid-1800s until 1895, when the state ordered their closure after a cave-in at the Tilly Foster mine killed thirteen men. Most of Connecticut's mines—such as Ore Hill in Salisbury, which was being mined as early as 1731—were in the northwestern part of the state.

Why did the ironworks last for so short a time? Perhaps the supply of good local ore was quickly exhausted. Maybe fuel was a problem; iron furnaces at the time required large quantities of charcoal, obtained by slowly burning wood in closed mounds. Trees for making charcoal were becoming less common as the area developed. Another possibility is that a competing ironworks at nearby Starrs Plain in Danbury ran the Ridgefield operation out of business.

Still another possibility is that the place burned down and wasn't worth replacing.

4

Nature, Wild and Tame

The Passing of the Pigeon

In nature, the passenger pigeon offers an example of how being plentiful doesn't necessarily guarantee survival, a fact that would have surprised a Ridgefield minister and his son two centuries ago.

Think of it: In 1800, passenger pigeons wandered the continent in unimaginable numbers—they were once the most plentiful birds in North America. Stories of immense flocks of them fill ornithological histories. In the early 1800s, an observer in Kentucky saw a single flock pass by that was some 240 miles long and 1 mile wide, estimated to contain more than two billion birds. In 1866, in Ontario, a mile-wide flock was reported to have taken fourteen hours to pass by and was said to contain more than *three billion* birds!

Such vast gatherings darkening the skies were not unusual until the late 1800s, when "pigeoners" finally began to seriously diminish the passenger pigeon population, enough to eventually do them in entirely. These pigeons were good eating, and their feathers were useful in stuffing mattresses and pillows. Pigeoners followed the flocks, using large nets to capture the birds, sometimes by the tens of thousands. At one point, one hundred barrels a day of pigeons were being shipped to the New York market alone.

And by 1914, they were gone. The last passenger pigeon died that year in a Cincinnati zoo.

Ridgefielders were once among the many who hunted the passenger pigeon. "The pigeons in spring and autumn migrated in countless flocks,

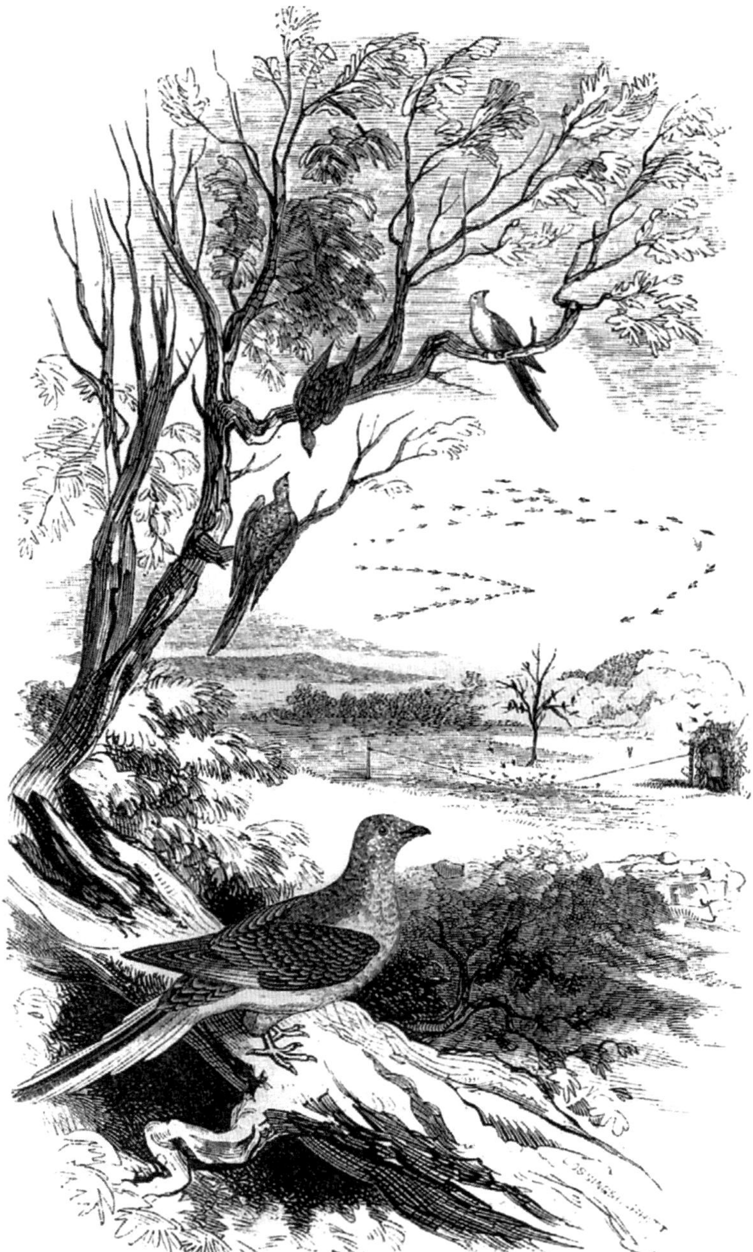

In his *Recollections of a Lifetime*, Samuel G. Goodrich provided an illustration of passenger pigeon netting. At mid-right of the background is the "bush hut" he and his father would hide in as they attracted the pigeons with "stool-birds." *From the author's collection.*

and many lingered in our woods for the season," wrote Samuel G. Goodrich ("Peter Parley"), describing Ridgefield life in the early 1800s. Goodrich recalled seeing "a stream of these noble birds, pouring at brief intervals through the skies, from the rising to the setting sun, and this in the county of Fairfield."

He admired the bird, which was still common in 1856 when he wrote these words: "Of all the pigeon tribe…the passenger pigeon is the swiftest and most beautiful of a swift and beautiful generation."

However, they were often hunted. "Game was, in point of fact, a substantial portion of the supply of food at certain seasons of the year," Goodrich said, adding that this species of pigeon was "unquestionably superior to any other for the table. All the other species of the eastern as well as the western continent, which I have tasted, are soft and flavorless in comparison."

Goodrich grew up on High Ridge, and he recalled the joys of pigeon hunting:

> *I can recollect no sports of my youth which equaled in excitement our pigeon hunts, generally taking place in September and October. We usually started on horseback before daylight, and made a rapid progress to some stubble-field on West Mountain. The ride in the keen, fresh air, especially as the dawn began to break, was delightful…My memory is still full of the sights and sounds of those glorious mornings: the silvery whistle of the wings of migrating flocks of plover—invisible in the gray mists of dawn; the faint murmur of the distant mountain torrents; the sonorous gong of the long-trailing flocks of wild geese, seeming to come from the unseen depths of the skies—these were among the suggestive sounds that stole through the dim twilight…*
>
> *Finally,* [he said, there was] *the rushing sound of the pigeons, pouring like a tide over the tops of the trees. By this time, of course, our nets were ready, and our flyers and stool-birds* [decoys] *on the alert. What moments of ecstasy were these, and especially when the head of the flock—some red-breasted old father or grandfather—caught the sight of our pigeons, and turning at the call, drew the whole train down into our net-bed. I have often seen a hundred, or two hundred of these splendid birds come upon us, with a noise absolutely deafening, and sweeping the air with a sudden gust, like the breath of a thundercloud.*

He added, "Sometimes our bush-hut, where we lay concealed, was covered all over with pigeons, and we dared not move a finger, as their red, piercing eyes were upon us. When at last, with a sudden pull of the rope, the net was sprung, and we went out to secure our booty—often fifty, and sometimes even a hundred birds—I felt a fullness of triumph, which words are wholly inadequate to express!"

Goodrich's father, Reverend S.G. Goodrich of the First Congregational Church, was an expert at netting pigeons. But sometimes, men of the cloth could run into problems with, of all things, men of the cloth.

The minister's son wrote in *Recollections of a Lifetime*:

> *One day, as I was with him on West Mountain, baiting pigeons. We had seduced a flock of three or four dozen down into the bed where they were feeding—my father and myself lying concealed in our bush-hut, close by.*
>
> *Suddenly, whang went a gun into the middle of the flock! Out we ran in great indignation, for at least a dozen of the birds were bleeding and fluttering before us. Scarcely had we reached the spot, when we met Parson M....of Lower Salem* [Lewisboro], *who had thus unwittingly poached upon us. The two clergymen had first a flurry and then a good laugh, after which they divided the plunder and parted.*

Both Goodriches, father and son, would be astounded to learn that a century later, the once plentiful passenger pigeon had passed away—permanently.

THE DEERLY DEPARTED

Deer had also been killed or driven out of Ridgefield long ago, among the "locally extinct" natives. And although these beautiful and docile creatures have managed to return, not everyone has been pleased with their more-than-successful comeback.

The white-tailed deer was much appreciated by the native Indians, who used our largest resident mammals for food and clothing and hunted and probably even trapped them. Back in the early 1700s, settlers named a location in the Bennett's Farm area "Buckspen Swamp." Daniel M. McKeon (1906–2001) reported that an old-timer once told him of the existence—in the woods off Great Hill Road—of a form of corral into which the Indians used to drive deer to trap and kill them for meat and hides. This was called a buckspen.

By the year 1800, deer were "extinct" in Ridgefield, according to Reverend Samuel Goodrich. The local population vanished probably because it was extensively hunted for food and because so much of its natural habitat was

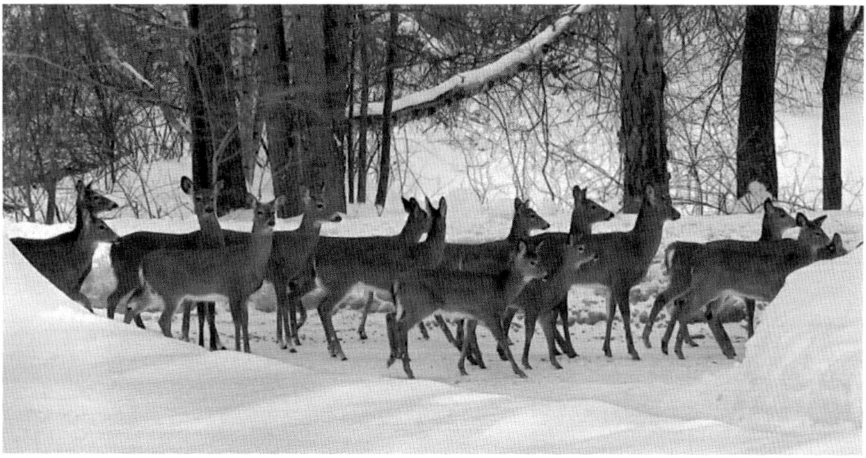

Ridgefielders a century or two ago would have been astounded to see this February 2011 scene: seventeen deer walking down Spectacle Lane. *Photograph by Deb and Tom Teitsworth, from the* Ridgefield Press *archives.*

destroyed as the settlers felled much of the town's forest to open the land for growing crops.

As Ridgefield moved from agrarian to bedroom community in the mid-twentieth century, the landscape began changing again. Trees returned in pockets of woodland throughout the town. This, mixed with lawns and fields, provided an ideal environment for the deer, which slowly began returning to town.

While even in the 1970s spotting a deer was fairly uncommon, all that had changed by the 1990s and the turn of the twenty-first century, when the town's deer population exploded. As many as eighty deer per square mile were being reported; the healthy density is said to be fifteen or fewer.

The overpopulating herbivores were causing all sorts of problems, from helping to foster and spread the ticks that carry Lyme disease to decimating the population of native field and woodland plants, particularly the forest understory. Perhaps worse, deer were involved in an incredible number of auto accidents. Around 2000, the Connecticut Department of Transportation said Ridgefield had the highest number of deer/vehicle accidents of any of the 169 towns in the entire state. Over the five years between April 2000 and May 2005, 883 deer were documented as killed in collisions with cars on or along Ridgefield's roads. The 883 were only the deer tagged by the Ridgefield Police and reported dead to the State of Connecticut; that total was estimated to be only a fraction of the actual number of deer hit by vehicles—many would wander off to die in the woods or continue living, maimed. And many motorists never bothered to report their accidents.

Some people were injured in crashes, but there were no known human fatalities here. In one of the worst accidents, a deer went through the windshield of a station wagon and wound up in the back seat. No one was seriously hurt. A cyclist required hospital treatment after his bicycle collided with a deer on North Salem Road.

After many months of study and deliberation, a selectmen-appointed panel of Ridgefielders recommended annual controlled "culling" of deer by hunters carefully selected by a town committee. The town-sponsored hunts have certainly cut down on their population. The deer numbers seem to have declined from their peak in the early 2000s, but other factors may also be involved in the decline, including a growing number of predators, such as coyotes and bobcats; some harsh winters; and even disease. Yet there are still plenty of deer around. A state helicopter survey of the town in February 2015 estimated there were still forty-five deer per square mile, well above the healthy density.

THE RETURN OF THE NATIVES

While the absent deer wandered back on their own, the wild turkey had to be trucked in.

Many turkeys were living in town when the settlers arrived—they love the forests and the foods the woods provided, especially acorns. By 1712, there was already a location in the Scotland District called "Turkey Island," probably because of the abundance of the birds in the area.

However, according to the state Department of Energy and Environmental Protection (DEEP), "a combination of forest clearing and a series of severe winters eliminated the turkey from Connecticut by the early 1800s."

From the 1950s into the 1970s, the state unsuccessfully tried to bring back the turkey through "artificial propagation"—catching them in other parts of the country and moving them here. "The major breakthrough in restoration efforts occurred when free-roaming Wild Turkeys were live-captured and translocated using a rocket net," DEEP said. "This large, lightweight net is fired by rockets from a remote blind and carried over turkeys that have been attracted to the area by bait."

Between 1975 and 1992, 356 wild turkeys were released at eighteen sites in all parts of Connecticut. Populations grew quickly in environments where trees had been allowed to return to the land, and by 1981, there were enough of the birds to allow the hunting of them. Today, DEEP says wild turkeys are found in all 169 towns and total between thirty-five and forty thousand birds. Connecticut has done so well at restoring the species that it has been helping other states reintroduce populations.

Ridgefield has plenty of turkeys. Especially in the spring and early summer, flocks of twenty-five or thirty birds wandering through yards are not uncommon. Their large numbers have prompted some to wonder whether turkeys, like deer, will overpopulate and start crashing into cars. However, turkey populations may be well held in balance by predators, such as coyotes, bobcats and fishers. What's more, turkeys seem smarter than deer when it comes to cars. I once was driving along a road in nearby Pound Ridge, New York, when a flock of turkeys decided to cross. The birds didn't walk, however, but took off and flew from one side to the other, just high enough to miss the cars that were passing beneath and just far enough to avoid the pavement.

Oddly enough, in the summer of 2014, I came across a lone wild turkey, standing on the side of South Olmstead Lane at 7:00 on a sunny morning, fast asleep. It was just barely off the travel portion of the highway, and never awoke as I stood there, taking pictures.

Probably because there were no turkeys in Fairfield County until recently, few turkey road names existed. Maybe, too, it was the fact that "turkey" has become a synonym for "jerk." Developers would jump for names like Cardinal Court, Partridge Drive or Pheasant Lane. But try "turkey," "crow" or even "vulture" on one of them, and you'd think someone had mentioned 20 percent mortgage rates.

However, when Robert Tuccio developed a new road at the Eleven Levels subdivision on West Mountain in the late 1970s, he named it Wild Turkey Court. Back in his younger, more skeptical days, this writer pooh-poohed the new name in the *Ridgefield Press*, noting that these birds had long been extinct in Connecticut and musing that the only wild turkey found in Ridgefield was in local package stores and liquor cabinets.

The next day, Tuccio showed up in the office with a photograph of a wild turkey taken just off Wild Turkey Court. Unbeknownst to the writer, the state had begun its restoration project and had been seeding West Mountain woods with turkeys. Indeed, Wild Turkey Court was a most appropriate name, marking the return of the native.

Not all state-sponsored returns have been greeted with cheers, however. The fisher, a member of the weasel family that can grow to three feet in length and weigh fourteen pounds, had been extirpated from the state by the year 1900, mostly because of over-trapping and because it lives in woodlands. Native populations remained in northern New England, and in 1988, the state DEEP began catching fishers in the north and reintroducing them in the northwestern Connecticut woods, with the aim of adding more fare for trappers who liked their fur. Within a few years, fishers were being spotted in Ridgefield, and they are now a resident species.

The problem with fishers, according to some observers, is that they can attack and eat domestic cats. However, experts feel that fishers are unlikely to go after most cats and that a far more dangerous predator is the coyote, a species that might once have been native and that reintroduced itself, without the state's help.

The Bluebirds of Happiness

A creature that has always been here—though it has suffered some declines—seems to be doing well and continues to bring joy to the winter-weary.

Two diaries of Ridgefielders who lived in the nineteenth century have been published. Their authors were about as different as two people could be. One was the sophisticated, well-read daughter of the village innkeeper and the other was a subsistence farmer and cobbler. One penned hundreds of long entries of her musings on the times while the other scratched out the brief basics of his day—weather, work, visitors, illnesses. But in one thing, at least, they were alike. While each wrote hardly anything about Ridgefield's wildlife, both recorded the annual arrival of bluebirds in late winter. For like little else in the cold days of February and early March, bluebirds presaged better times ahead: the coming of spring and a more comfortable and productive climate.

On March 7, 1865, farmer Jared Nash reported: "Clear. Cut some wood. Our folks went up to Jared's in afternoon. Bluebirds come today." On February 22 the following year, he wrote: "Clear and pleasant. We work at wood. Gathered things to make a syrup for Emmie. Quite muddy. Bluebirds came."

Jared lived in the south of town, on Silver Spring Road (at the border of today's Silver Spring Country Club), good territory for seeing bluebirds, which love wide-open fields. But up in the village, Anna Marie Resseguie also paid attention to the arrival of these striking birds, although her reports were aural rather than visual.

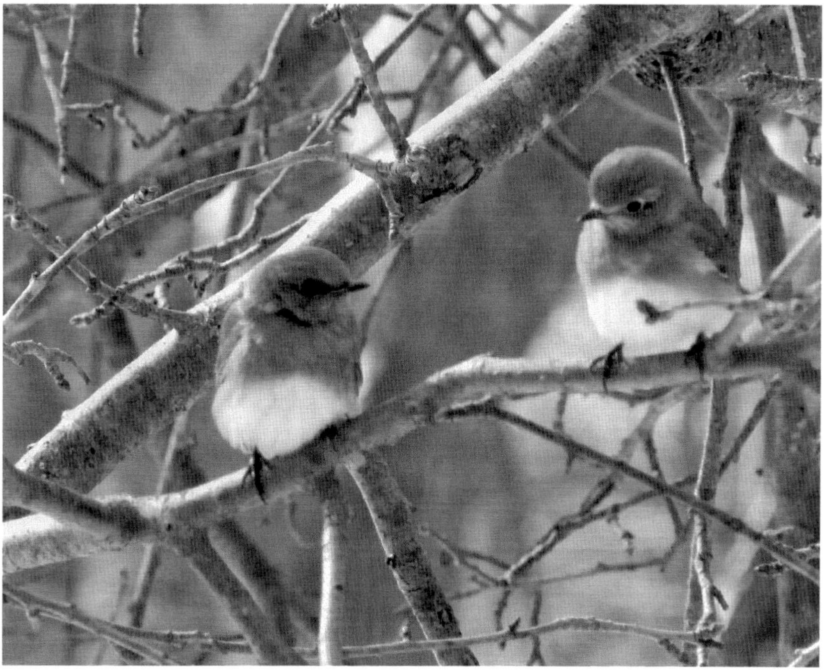

For Ridgefielders in the eighteenth and nineteenth centuries, the appearance of bluebirds in February or early March was a sign of better days to come. Today, many stay year-round. *Photograph by the author.*

"Phillis hears bluebirds sing this morning," she wrote on March 11, 1862. On March 11, 1865, she said: "I heard bluebirds for the first time Monday the 6th." She beat Jared by a day that year. Anna was the daughter of Abijah and Anna Keeler Resseguie, who operated what we today call the Keeler Tavern on Main Street. She lived at the tavern with her parents and Phillis Dubois, a black woman who, as a child, had been freed from slavery and had become a part of the Resseguie family.

Back then, bluebirds heralded spring's arrival, much more so than the robins seem to today. Their appearance on March 6 and 7 indicates the winter of 1865 might have been harsher on wildlife than that of 1866, when Jared noted their arrival on February 22.

Bluebirds were much more common in the nineteenth century before the importation of European species that chased many of these natives from their nesting holes in trees. The territory then was more bluebird friendly, too: the fields and orchards common in the area provided plenty of open space, which they favor.

Wise farmers loved birds and went out of their way to attract them. Many species eat the larvae or adult forms of insects that attack many of the crops the farmers grew. Others feasted on the seeds of weeds that stole nutrients from their fields. Many farmers maintained flocks of pigeons to eat pest insects and weed seeds and also encouraged wild birds by making birdhouses of dried, hollowed squashes and hanging scores of them from orchard trees. An old straw hat, nailed open-side out to the side of a barn, could attract nesting wrens, which are ravenous insect-eaters.

Today, many people build or buy nesting boxes, and efforts have been so extensive and widespread that the bluebird population has been increasing in the Northeast. "With the proliferation of nest boxes and bluebird trails [series of boxes], bluebirds are now a common sight along roads, field edges, golf courses, and other open areas," says Cornell University's Lab of Ornithology.

Because of the generally milder winters today, many bluebirds (robins, too) stay in Ridgefield year-round, gathering in flocks and spending the cold months in wetlands and woods, feeding on berries and seeds. During the dead of winter, bluebirds practice an interesting technique for keeping warm at night. A few years ago, a local correspondent told me how she witnessed it:

> *Recently, on a day when outside looked very white as snow was falling and already covering the ground, my husband and I witnessed a burst of color. Late in the afternoon, we saw about eight bluebirds sitting in the tree near our birdfeeders. Much to our surprise, some of them visited our feeders. This was our first experience at seeing bluebirds do this so we knew they must be very hungry. Most interesting, however, was what happened as the sun set. We witnessed a well-organized entry into a bluebird house at the edge of our yard. At least five of the birds seemed to squeeze themselves into the little house. Since that evening, we have observed this behavior several more times.*

A number of cold-weather species practice communal "bundling," as the old New Englanders called snuggling on a cold winter's night, but this was the first time I'd heard of bluebirds doing it.

Ridgefielders with feeders that use hulled sunflower seeds (also called sunflower seed "hearts") can have bluebirds in their yards throughout January and February, snow or no snow. Having a bluebird box or two in the yard also helps attract them. And how nice it is in January to have this colorful reminder that spring will soon come.

The Hoop Pole of Old

The vegetable world has been the source of much benefit in many ways. But mention a "hoop pole" today, and one might inspire images of basketball or tent supports or just a blank stare. A century or two ago, however, hoop poles were a well-known and valuable commodity that some Ridgefield farmers harvested from the wild and perhaps from dedicated fields to earn extra cash.

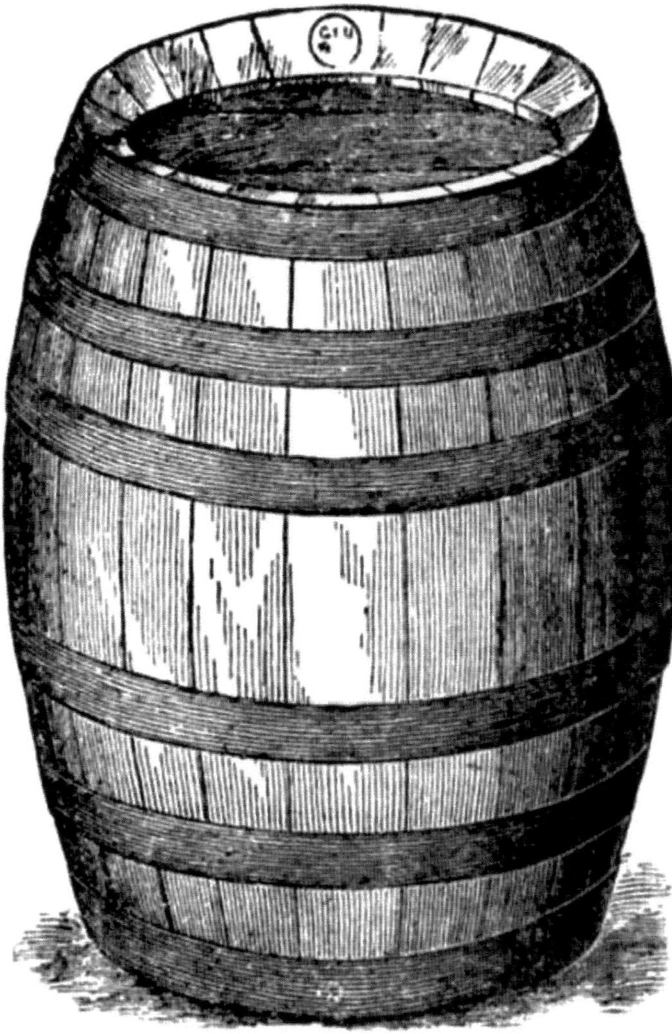

Old barrels were held together with hoops, made from hoop poles. *From the author's collection.*

Hoop poles were long, straight rods, cut in the woods from ash, hickory, pignut, hazel and white oak saplings or from bushes that had been specially pruned for the purpose. Some poles were used around the farm as rollers for moving heavy loads and for temporary floors under haystacks. Some were split up and employed in basket weaving. Perhaps the oddest use for hoop poles was as stiffeners in the colossal skirts fashionable women wore in the nineteenth century.

However, most hoop poles were used to make barrels, providing the bands or "hoops" that hold the barrel sides or staves together.

Hoop wood was cut in the fall, but farmers usually processed it in winter, when they had finished their work in the crop fields. The poles were split into two to five strips, depending on the diameter of the pole and the quality of the wood. Bark and shoots had to be shaved off. Sometimes the poles were hammered to flatten them.

They were then bundled in packages of one hundred for sale, some to local barrel makers and others to the large New York City market. While barrels today are mostly used as decorative items, they were the main method of packaging raw goods in the nineteenth century and earlier.

Certain kinds of hoop wood were used for certain kinds of barrels, depending on their strength. A hoop pole farmer in Ulster County, New York, told the *New York Times* in 1893: "The best hoops are the hickory and pignut. These are used for apple, pork, vinegar, and beef barrels, kegs and other classes of fine cooperage." Oak was used to strap packing boxes. Mountain ash was favored for "butter tubs, firkins, and flour and sugar barrels." Chestnut was used only for gunpowder kegs. The poorest quality wood was used for hooping cement and lime barrels.

Today, other methods, such as cardboard boxes, metal containers and tanks, cans and bottles, have replaced the functions of the old-fashioned barrel. Before the barrel disappeared as a container, however, the wooden hoop had faded from the scene as barrel-makers found iron straps stronger.

To a nineteenth-century farmer, hoops could be a valuable source of some extra cash. A bundle of shaved hoops for cement and lime barrels could bring about $0.50 cents while the stronger hickory and oak straps used for packing boxes could fetch $3.00 ($75.00 in 2015 money). Some serious hoop farmers could earn close to $2,000.00 ($50,000.00 today) in a season, according to the *Times* article.

Since hoop poles were of value, they could also be the targets of the unscrupulous. In his diary, Silver Spring Road farmer Jared Nash reported on February 8, 1865, "S. Hurlbutt called to summons Father to go up to court tomorrow to take up J. Bennett for cutting hooppoles. Hurlbutt call after bedtime and told Father he need not go, for Jerry had settled it."

While there were no other details, it appears that Sereno Hurlbutt, a local constable, had summoned Jeremiah "Jere" (or "Jerry") Bennett for illegally cutting hoop poles on someone else's property. Jared's father was to bring Jere to court. However, as with so many cases today, Bennett and the plaintiff had apparently agreed at the last minute to "settle out of court."

BIG TREES AND THEIR SWEETS

Nature offers many forms of arboreal bounty, not the least of which is the sugar maple.

Ridgefield's Notable Trees, a guide published by the town's Tree Committee, points out that the sugar maple produces one of the most valuable lumber and furniture hardwoods. But hereabouts, this species is especially famous for its syrup. "To gather the sap used for maple syrup, New England's sugar maples are tapped in late winter or early spring before the buds of the tree begin to swell," the booklet says. "It takes 40 gallons of crude sap boiled down to make one gallon of maple syrup."

In his *Recollections of a Lifetime*, Samuel G. Goodrich ("Peter Parley") says that around the year 1800, household sugar was "partially supplied by our maple-trees. These were tapped in March, the sap being collected, and boiled down in the woods. This was wholly a domestic operation, and one in which all the children rejoiced, each taking his privilege of an occasional sip or dip, from the period of the limpid sap, to the granulated condiment. Nevertheless, the chief supply of sugar was from the West Indies."

A few people in Ridgefield today still go through the trouble of tapping trees and boiling sap. But at least one couple I know gave it up after the first year they tried. They boiled and boiled the sap on their kitchen stove, producing so much steam that the wallpaper began peeling off their household walls. They decided to keep the paper and buy the syrup.

The maple nowadays is appreciated more for its appearance than its flavor. But its beauty was always enjoyed. Goodrich offered this view of Main Street in the 1850s when he was visiting his old hometown: "The street, on the whole, is one of the most beautiful I know of. It is more than a mile in length and a hundred and twenty feet in width, ornamented with two continuous lines of trees—elms, sycamores, and sugar-maples—save only

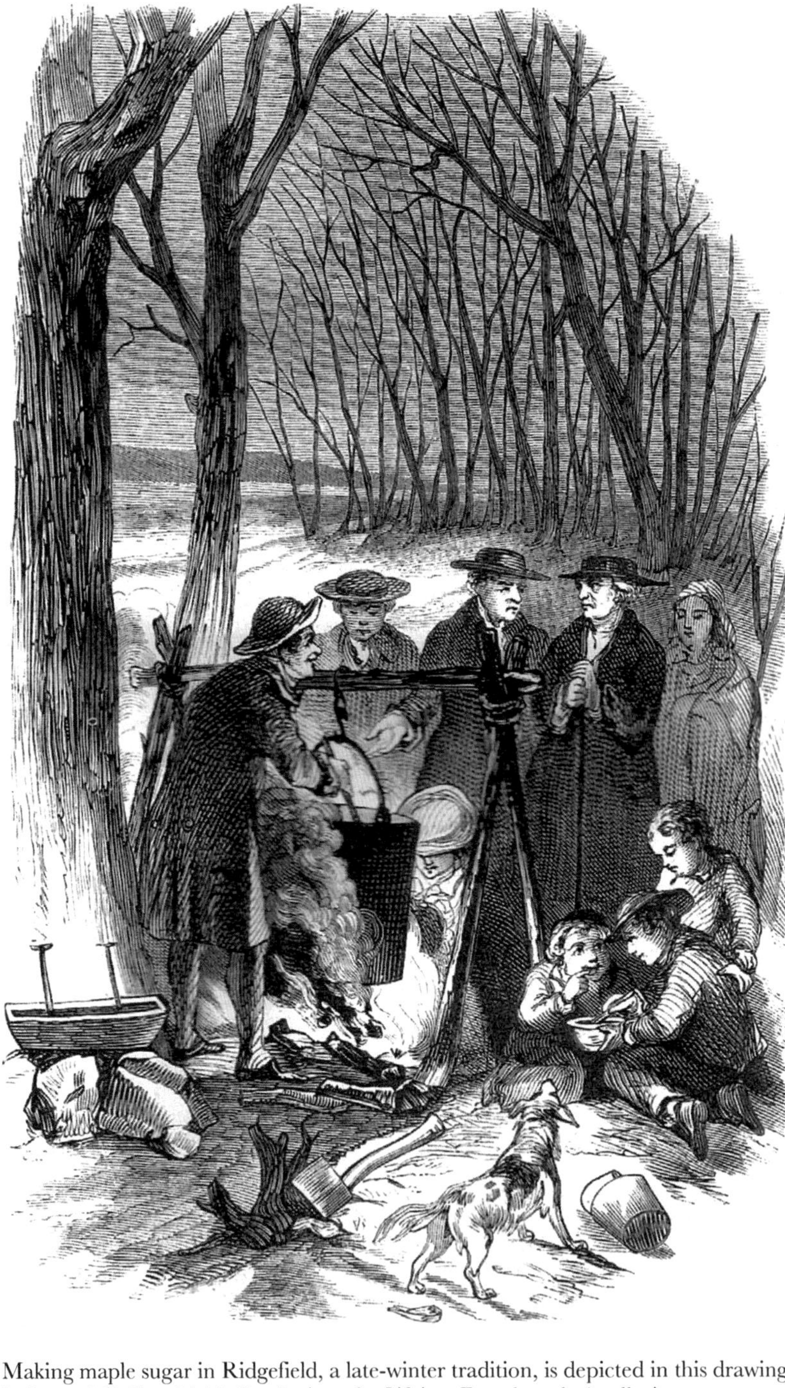

Making maple sugar in Ridgefield, a late-winter tradition, is depicted in this drawing in Samuel G. Goodrich's *Recollections of a Lifetime. From the author's collection.*

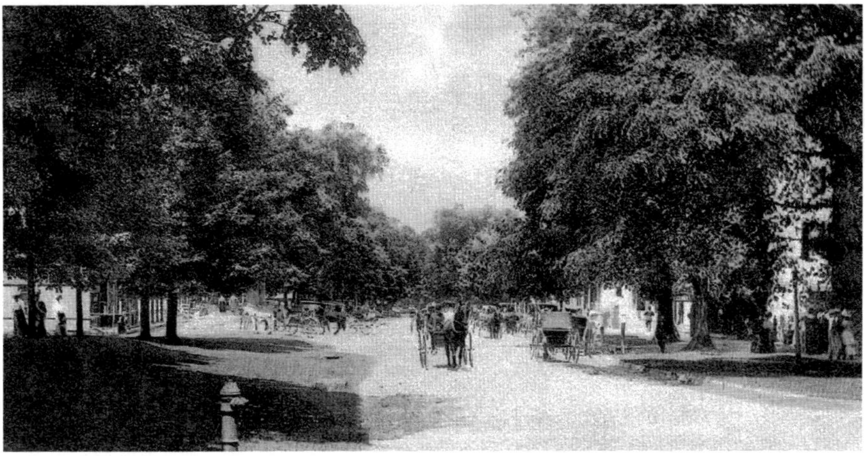

Trees dominated the center of town a century ago. This view from about 1905 looks north on Main Street from Governor Street. *Postcard in author's collection.*

here and there a brief interval. Some of these, in front of the more imposing houses, are truly majestic."

Unfortunately, time has been taking its toll on the majestic village trees. For instance, until recently, many people who walked the tree-lined sidewalks of Main Street would happen upon a sign near the Aldrich Museum that said a tree there was the third-largest sugar maple in Ridgefield. The sign is gone now, and so is the tree, chopped down by the state highway department in the winter of 2015 because it was dying and a hazard.

The sign made people wonder: if this was the third-largest sugar maple, where are the first and second largest?

The sign was result of the "Ridgefield's Largest Sugar Maple Contest" in 2008, the year of the town's 300th anniversary celebration. Sponsored by the town's Tree Committee, the contest marked Ridgefield's tercentennial by noting some of its oldest living inhabitants: the trees.

However, dating a tree is difficult unless it's cut down and the growth rings are counted. Measuring size is easier, and the committee employed a formula, used by foresters, that produces a rating for overall size of tree, based on height, trunk circumference and average spread.

The first-place winner is still standing on southern Main Street—near Number 57 on the west side, opposite Rockwell Road. A sign placed there disappeared long ago, but a new one appeared in the spring of 2015. Nicholas Molyneux, then nine, spotted it and received a $300 check at the contest's awards ceremony on June 28, 2008, in Ballard

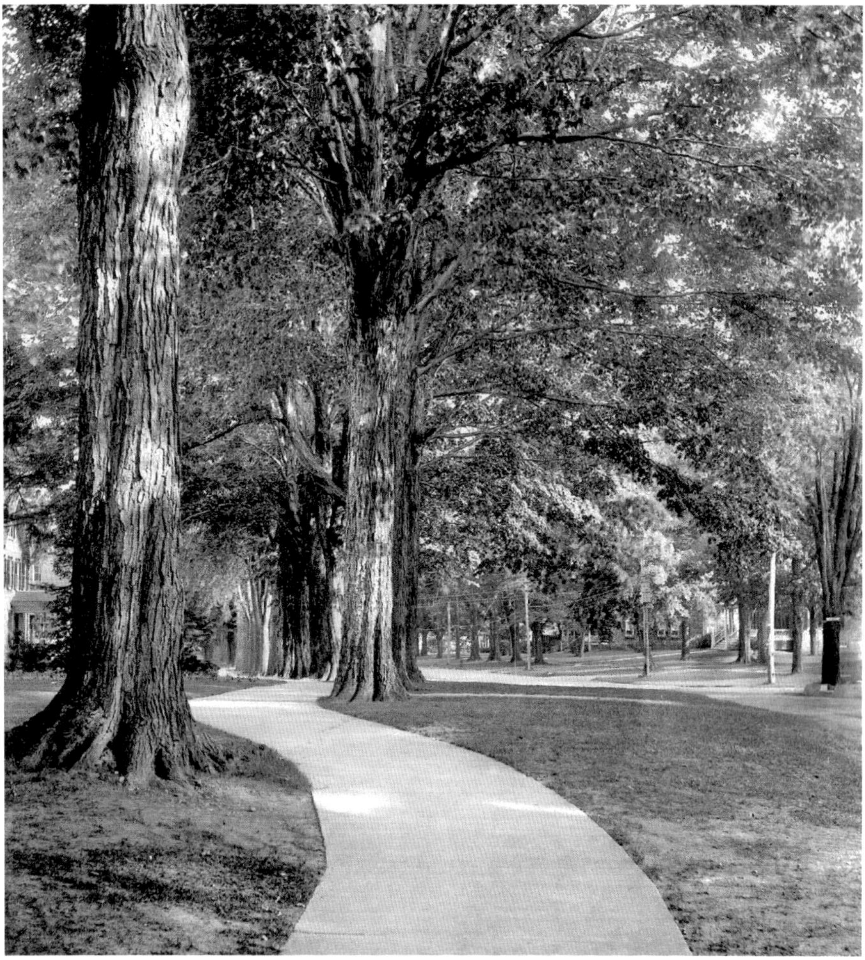

This view shows the sidewalk on the east side of Main Street in the 1920s or early 1930s, looking south from near the Keeler Tavern Museum. There are still many trees today, but they are not quite as majestic as these. *From the* Ridgefield Press *archives.*

Park. According to *Ridgefield's Notable Trees*, this maple was ninety-five feet tall with a trunk circumference of sixteen feet, six inches, and an average spread of eighty-four feet, six inches. And that was in 2008—it's undoubtedly bigger now.

The second-place winner was also spotted by a youngster, Frank Maiorino, who found it in the old Titicus Cemetery. "Frank had earlier withdrawn his first entry when a huge limb on his family's large sugar maple had to be removed to protect his house—he and his mother then went to the cemetery near their house to search for another entry," said Nancy Boersma, former chairman of the Tree Committee. Jack got $200.

The third-place winner ($100) was Valerie Jensen, whose home was shaded by that tree, which, alas, is now gone.

A PACHYDERM PLACE?

Elephants once roamed Ridgefield, and at least one might be buried there.

There's a lane in Ridgebury called Schoolhouse Place. The dead-end road off northern Ridgebury Road serves Paul McNamara's 1981 seven-lot subdivision of the former Lee B. Wood property. When he proposed the development to the Planning and Zoning Commission, Attorney McNamara suggested that the road be called Woods Court, a punny name that zoning officials thought would be too easily confused with roads like Woodland Way, Woodlawn Drive, Woodstone Road and Woody Place.

This writer, then the town's OAMTN (official advisor on municipal thoroughfare nomenclature), was asked for his thoughts. The OAMTN reported that circus pioneer Aaron Turner—whose life was described in *Ridgefield Chronicles*—owned that property in the nineteenth century and, some say, kept elephants and other exotic animals on or near the tract. Various four-legged circus stars would spend the winter on Ridgebury farms, sleeping in barns and roaming in fields. In fact, at least one elephant is supposed to have been buried on or near the Wood property.

So, half in jest, "Pachyderm Place" was suggested.

Too ponderous, came the reply.

Maybe "Three-Ring Circle"? someone else suggested.

Too cutesy.

A zoning official suggested Big Top Lane, but that sounded too much like a loaf of bread (who today remembers Big Top Bread?).

Finally, Commissioner Daniel M. McKeon, a longtime Ridgeburian and student of its history, offered Schoolhouse Place. McKeon said the new road would connect to Ridgebury Road very near the site of the old North Ridgebury Schoolhouse, then represented by only the ruins of a foundation.

North Ridgebury was one of the last school districts to get a schoolhouse. An 1867 map shows no schoolhouse there, although there were district lines, suggesting that for a long time, residents of this district had sent their children to a schoolhouse to the north in nearby Danbury (territory that, until 1846, was part of Ridgefield).

In 1871, the estate of Aaron Turner, dead by then, sold to "School District Number 15 of Ridgefield" an eight- by ten-rod (half-acre) tract on the west side Ridgebury Road with the proviso that the school district make and keep forever "a tight stone fence five feet high" between the Turner land and the schoolhouse land.

Was the fence designed to keep schoolchildren off the Turner land or Turner animals away from the schoolchildren? It was probably the latter so the Turner heirs would not be liable for one of its animals hurting a child. However, the animals were probably just cows—by then, there was no threat of injury by an errant elephant!

Our African Side

At 6:07 a.m. on the morning of October 19, 1985, Ridgefielders who were awake—and those who were awakened—felt something unusual. Their homes were shaking; dishes rattled a bit, pictures tilted a tad, old plaster may even have cracked. They were experiencing the effects of the first significant earthquake in the New York metropolitan area in a century.

Centered near Ardsley, New York, in neighboring Westchester County, the quake registered 4.0 on the Richter scale. The previous major earthquake, in 1884, measured 5.0. There was no significant damage in Ridgefield and little elsewhere, though a New York town reported some cracked pavement.

However, the quake brought to light a geological phenomenon that had been little known outside scientific circles and that affected the very foundation, literally, of Ridgefield. The quake was strongly felt along "Cameron's Line," a fault that runs from Manhattan northeasterly through Westchester and into Ridgefield. Here, the line enters near the southwest corner of town and almost exactly follows West Lane and High Ridge into the village. It continues across Prospect Ridge through Great Swamp and Farmingville. Then the line heads into Redding, up to Danbury and northerly into Litchfield County.

But Cameron's Line is no run-of-the-mill fault. As veteran science reporter Walter Sullivan explained it in the *New York Times* the day after the quake, the line "marks an abrupt change in the earth's crust that resulted from a collision between North America and a European-African land mass 400

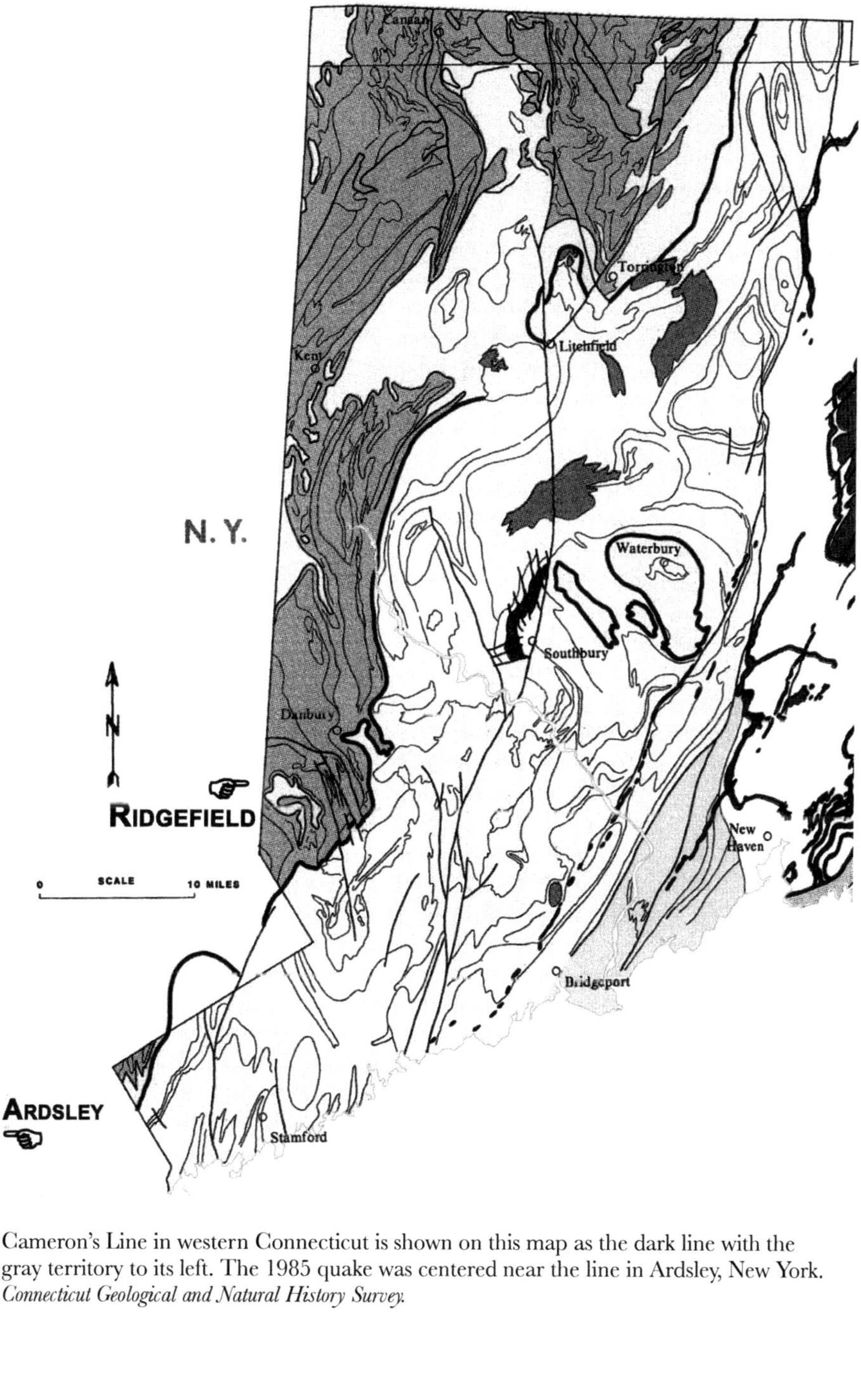

Cameron's Line in western Connecticut is shown on this map as the dark line with the gray territory to its left. The 1985 quake was centered near the line in Ardsley, New York. *Connecticut Geological and Natural History Survey.*

million years ago." Later, the European-African continent pulled away, leaving behind a piece of its edge. Geologists with the Hudson Institute of Mineralogy describe the result this way: "The rocks south of the Cameron's Line are mostly Ordovician unnamed felsic orthogneiss with some of the Harrison Gneiss metadiorite in the Branchville area. North of Cameron's Line, higher elevations with rugged topography along the eastern, northern and western part of town (such as under Pine, Ned, and West Mountains), are underlain by Grenville age Laurentian gneiss bedrock."

More simply put, if you live in the southern third of town, the earth beneath you closely matches the geology of today's western Africa while folks in the northern two-thirds of the town live atop North American rock.

Mild quakes, the kind most people would not even feel, occur fairly often along Cameron's Line and many other faults in the region. The 1985 quake in Ardsley was actually centered two miles west of the line, but it was felt along the fault on up into western Massachusetts. Connecticut as a state has several earthquakes a year, but they are below 2.5 on the Richter scale and generally not felt. The area around Moodus, in eastern Connecticut, is famed for its "rumblings" and has experienced a series of up to four hundred quakes over six weeks, mostly too small to feel. (Native Indians called East Haddam, the next town south, *morehemoodus*, "place of noises.")

In October 1989, the Loma Prieta earthquake in California registered 6.9, killed 63 people, injured 3,700 and damaged 12,000 homes and 2,600 businesses. Forty buildings collapsed in Santa Cruz. A week later, scientists told the *Ridgefield Press* that the town could experience an earthquake "with the level of violence and…havoc" of the California quake. Here, however, the damage would be even worse than an equivalent shock in California, both because most buildings haven't been designed with quakes in mind and because the crust of the earth is more solid and better able to transmit and maintain the magnitude of earthquake waves than the softer ground of the West Coast. That same year, the state passed building codes incorporating the need for seismic designs, but many older buildings—such as most of our schools and the town hall—are brittle brick and/or cement block structures that don't do well in quakes (wooden houses are the safest).

There are many faults that crisscross the metropolitan New York region, and scientists seem uncertain about the level of danger they may present. The faults are certainly not as active as California's. Back in 1985, Columbia University seismologists said the October 19 quake might have been a warning of a more severe quake to come within months. "They stressed, however, that this was a possibility, rather than a probability, and other specialists expressed doubts regarding the prognosis," said the *Times*.

In 2011, the 5.8 earthquake in Virginia that damaged the Washington Monument was felt in Ridgefield (and across twelve states and southern Canada). But as of this writing, no local quakes like Arsley's has occurred since 1985. And for most of us, that's just fine.

Bibliography

Ables, Kay, et al. *A View from the Inn: The Journal of Anna Marie Resseguie 1851–1867*. Ridgefield, CT: Keeler Tavern Preservation Society Inc., 1993.

Bailey, James Montgomery. *History of Danbury, Conn. 1684–1896*. New York: Burr Printing House, 1896.

Bedini, Silvio A. *Ridgefield in Review*. Ridgefield, CT: 250th Anniversary Committee, 1958.

Cornwall, L. Peter. *In the Shore Line's Shadow: The Six Lives of the Danbury & Norwalk Railroad*. Littleton, MA: Flying Yankee Enterprises, 1987.

DeLuca, Richard. *Post Roads and Iron Horses: Transportation in Connecticut from Colonial Times to the Age of Steam*. Middletown, CT: Wesleyan University Press, 2011.

Goodrich, Samuel G. *The Animal Kingdom Illustrated*. New York: A.J. Johnson, 1874 edition.

———. *Recollections of a Lifetime*. New York: Miller, Orton and Mulligan, 1856.

Haight, Robert S. *St. Stephen's Church, Ridgefield, Connecticut, Its History for 250 Years*. Ridgefield, CT, 1975.

Hall, Reverend Edwin. *The Ancient Historical Records of Norwalk, Conn*. Norwalk, CT: James Mallory & Co., 1847. Reprint, Norwalk, CT: Friends of the Lockwood House, 1973.

Hambrick-Stowe, Dr. Charles. *We Gather Together: Making the Good News Happen 1712–2012*. Ridgefield, CT: First Congregational Church, 2011.

Holbrook, Stewart H. *The Old Post Road*. American Trails Series. New York: McGraw-Hill, 1962.

Huden, John C. *Indian Place Names of New England.* New York: Museum of the American Indian Heye Foundation, 1962.

Hurd, D. Hamilton. *History of Fairfield County*. Philadelphia: J.W. Lewis & Co., 1881.

Jackson, S. Trevena. *Fanny Crosby's Story of Ninety-Four Years*. New York: Fleming H. Revell Company, 1915.

Jones, Keith Marshall, III. *The Farms of Farmingville*. Ridgefield: Connecticut Colonel Press, 2001.

Jordan, Alvin R., et al. *A History of the Town of Lewisboro*. South Salem, NY: Lewisboro History Book Committee, 1981.

Land Records and Vital Records, Town of Ridgefield, 1708–1900.

Nash, Jared. *Diary, 1865–66*. Edited by Jack Sanders. RidgefieldHistory.com, 1995.

Nevins, Allan. *An Historical Sketch of Ridgefield*. Ridgefield, CT: Elms Inn, n.d. (reported to be 1920s).

Ridgefield Archives Committee. *Images of America: Ridgefield*. Mount Pleasant, SC: Arcadia Publishing, 1999.

Ridgefield Press, 1875–2015.

Robinson, Solon. *Facts for Farmers*. 2 vols. New York: A.J. Johnson, 1866.

Rockwell, George L. *The History of Ridgefield, Connecticut*. Ridgefield, CT: privately printed by the author, 1927.

Sanders, Jack. *Five Village Walks*. 3rd ed. Ridgefield, CT: Ridgefield Historical Society, 2008.

———. *Notable Ridgefielders*. Ridgefield, CT: Ridgefield Press, 2000.

———. *Ridgefield Chronicles*. Charleston, SC: The History Press, 2014.

———. *Ridgefield Names*. Ridgefield, CT: RidgefieldHistory.com, 1995.

———. *Ridgefield 1900–1950*. Postcard History Series. Mount Pleasant, SC: Arcadia Publishing, 2003.

Savell, Isabelle Keating. *Daughter of Vermont: A Biography of Emily Eaton Hepburn*. New York: North River Press, 1952.

Stewart, George R. *American Place Names*. New York: Oxford University Press, 1970.

Teller, Reverend Daniel W. *The History of Ridgefield, Conn*. Danbury, CT: T. Donovan, 1878.

Todd, Charles Burr. *The History of Redding, Connecticut*. New York: Grafton Press, 1906.

Welsh, Glenna M. *The Proprietors of Ridgefield*. Ridgefield, CT: Caudatowa Press, 1976.

Wood, Frederic J. *The Turnpikes of New England*. Boston: Marshall Jones Company, 1919.

Index

K

L

M

N

O

P

R

S

T

V

W

About the Author

A Connecticut native and Holy Cross graduate, Jack Sanders retired in 2014 after forty-three years as an editor of the *Ridgefield Press*, a 140-year-old community newspaper in Connecticut. His books of history and natural history include *Ridgefield Chronicles* (The History Press), *Ridgefield 1900–1950* (Arcadia), *The Secrets of Wildflowers* (Lyons) and *Hedgemaids and Fairy Candles* (McGraw-Hill). He and his wife, Sally, also a newspaper editor, live in a 250-year-old farmhouse in Ridgefield, enjoy bicycling and have two sons.

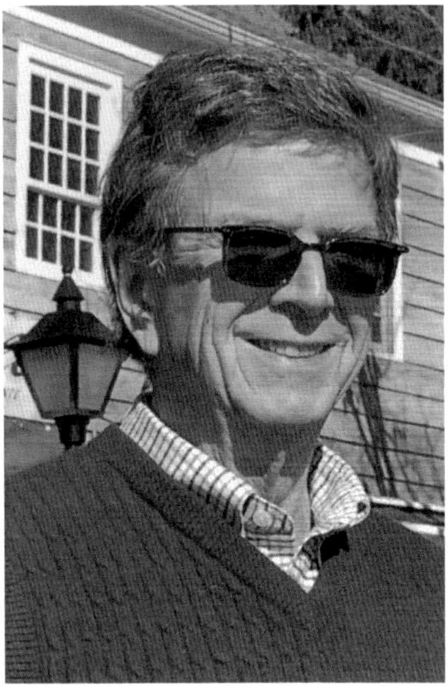

Photograph by Macklin Reid, the *Ridgefield Press*.